1926

William Hilburn $2.00

THE

AMERICAN VIGNOLA

PART I

THE FIVE ORDERS

By WILLIAM R. WARE

FORMERLY PROFESSOR OF ARCHITECTURE IN MASSACHUSETTS INSTITUTE OF TECHNOLOGY
EMERITUS PROFESSOR OF ARCHITECTURE IN COLUMBIA UNIVERSITY

FIFTH EDITION

SCRANTON

INTERNATIONAL TEXTBOOK COMPANY

1926

Press of
International Textbook Company
Scranton, Pa.

21932

PREFACE

IN January, 1859, I went from Mr. Edward Cabot's office in Boston, where I had been for two or three years, to join the little company of half a dozen young men who were studying architecture in the Studio Building in Tenth Street, under the inspiration of Mr. Richard Hunt. Mr. Hunt had just returned from Paris and was eager to impart to younger men, though we were not much his juniors, what he had learned in the *Ecole des Beaux-Arts* and in work upon the New Louvre. We had all, I believe, had more or less of office experience, but those were the days when the Gothic Revival was at its height, and Mr. Hunt found most of us unfamiliar with Classical details and quite unskilled in their use. I, at any rate, knew hardly a touch of them, and I remember well the day when, as I was carefully drawing out a Doric Capital according to the measurements given in my *Vignola*, Mr. Hunt took the pencil out of my hand and, setting aside the whole apparatus of *Modules* and *Minutes*, showed me how to divide the height of my Capital into thirds, and those into thirds, and those again into thirds, thus getting the sixths, ninths, eighteenths, twenty-sevenths, and fifty-fourths of a Diameter which the rules required, without employing any larger divisor than two or three.

It seemed as if this method, so handy with the Doric Capital, might be applied to other things, and I forthwith set myself to studying the details of all the Orders, and to devising for my own use simple rules for drawing them out. The present work presents the results of these endeavors. Experience in the class room has, meanwhile, amplified and extended them, and they have at many points been improved by the suggestions of my colleagues.

I am particularly indebted to Professor Hamlin and to Mr. W. T. Partridge for some ingenious applications of the 45-degree line to the Doric Entablature and to the Corinthian Capital, and for an analogous employment of the 60-degree line.

Finding that the plates in which, for the convenience of my own students, I have embodied these results are somewhat in demand by others, I now publish them in the present volume, adding such text and marginal illustrations as the subject matter seems to require. The Plates have been drawn out for me anew by Mr. Partridge, as have also most of the Illustrations. The rest have been taken from standard publications, especially from Bühlmann's "*Architecture of Classical Antiquity and the Renaissance*," which has furnished twenty-six of the Figures.

The forms and proportions here set forth are, in the main, those worked out by Giacomo Barozzi da Vignola and first published by him at Rome in the year 1563, as those which, in his judgment, best embodied the best practice of the ancient Romans. Other systems have been presented by Alberti, Palladio, Scamozzi, Serlio, Sir William Chambers, and others. But Vignola's Orders have generally been accepted as the standard. His works have been frequently republished, and recourse must be had to them for minute information in regard to details. But the dimensions given in this book, and the methods of determining them here described, will suffice for the execution of all drawings and designs which are made to a small scale.

This volume is concerned only with Columns, Pilasters and Entablatures, Pediments, Pedestals, and Balustrades. The employment of these Elements in the Composition of Doors and Windows, Wall Surfaces,

iii

external and internal, Staircases, Towers, and Spires, Arches and Arcades, Vaults and Domes, and other architectural features, will, I hope, at a later day be made the subject of a separate treatise which will be the natural sequel to this one.

After the chief part of this volume was in press my attention was directed to a somewhat similar work by the celebrated James Gibbs, the architect of St. Martin's-in-the-Fields and of St. Mary-le-Strand. He published in London, in 1732, a series of plates showing the Orders and their applications with a brief descriptive text. The title page reads: "Rules for Drawing the Several Parts of Architecture in a more Exact and Easy Manner than has been heretofore Practiced, by which all Fractions, in dividing the Principal Members and their Parts, are Avoided." The book begins with an *Address to the Reader* which opens as follows:

"Upon examination of the common ways of drawing the Five Orders of Architecture, I thought there might be a method found out so to divide the principal Members and their Parts, both as to their Heights and Projections, as to avoid Fractions. And having tried one Order with success, I proceeded to another, till at length I was satisfied it would answer my intention in all; and I doubt not but that the Method here proposed will be acknowledged by proper Judges to be the most exact, as well as the easiest, that hath as yet been published."

I find on examining the plates that, though they follow an entirely different system, they have anticipated some of the methods of the present work.

WILLIAM R. WARE.

October 1, 1902.
SCHOOL OF ARCHITECTURE, COLUMBIA UNIVERSITY.

CONTENTS

THE AMERICAN VIGNOLA

The Five Orders

INTRODUCTION

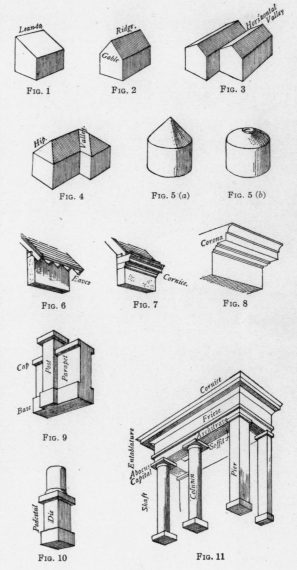

A BUILDING is a shelter from rain, sun, and wind. This implies a *Roof*, and *Walls* to support it. If the walls entirely enclose the space within, there are *Doorways* for access, and *Windows* for light. Roofs and walls, doors and windows are the essential features of buildings.

Roofs may be flat, sloping, or curved. A roof with one slope is called a *Lean-to*, Fig. 1. When two sloping roofs rest upon parallel walls and lean against one another, they meet in a horizontal *Ridge*, Fig. 2, at the top, and form a *Gable* at each end. Roofs that rise from the same wall in opposite directions form a *Horizontal Valley*, Fig. 3, at the wall. If two walls make a projecting angle, their roofs intersect in an inclined line called a *Hip*, Fig. 4. If the walls meet in a reentering angle, the inclined line of intersection is called a *Valley*. Circular walls carry conical, Fig. 5 (*a*) or domical roofs, Fig. 5 (*b*).

If there is more than one story, the flat roof of the lower story becomes the *Floor* of the story above. If the roof extends beyond the wall that supports it, the projection is called the *Eaves*, Fig. 6. If the wall also projects, to support the extension of the roof, the projection is called a *Cornice*, Fig. 7. The principal member of a cornice, which projects like a shelf and crowns the wall, is called a *Corona*, Fig. 8.

Walls are generally made wider just at the bottom, so as to get a better bearing on the ground. This projection is the *Base*, Fig. 9. A similar projection at the top is called a *Cap*, or, if it projects much, a *Cornice*, as has been said. A low wall is called a *Parapet*. A short piece of wall about as long as it is thick is called a *Post*, and if it supports something, a *Pedestal*, Fig. 10, the part between its Cap and Base is then the *Die*. A tall post is called a *Pier*, Fig. 11, if it is square, and a *Column* if it is round. Caps of piers and columns are called *Capitals*, and the part between the Cap and the Base, the *Shaft*. The flat upper member of a Capital is called the *Abacus*.

1

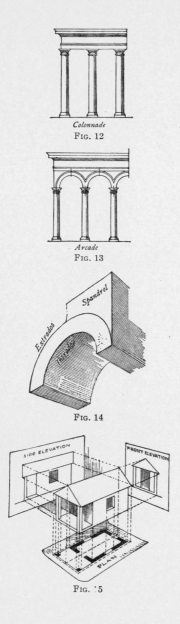

Colonnade
FIG. 12

Arcade
FIG. 13

FIG. 14

FIG. 15

A beam that spans the space between two piers or columns, or between a pier or column and a wall, is called an *Architrave*, or *Epistyle*. Above it, between the Architrave and the Cornice, there is generally a little strip of wall called the *Frieze*. Architrave, Frieze, and Cornice constitute the *Entablature*. A series of columns is called a *Colonnade*, Fig. 12. The spaces between piers or columns are sometimes spanned by *Arches*, a series of which is called an *Arcade*, Fig. 13.

The space between two parallel walls is sometimes covered by a sort of continuous arch, called a *Vault*, instead of by a floor or roof, Fig. 14.

The under surface of a beam or architrave is called its *Soffit*, and the same name is used also for the *Intrados*, or under surface of an arch or vault. The upper surface, or back of an arch, is called the *Extrados*, and the triangular space of wall above is called a *Spandrel*.

The Wall, the Pier, and the Column, with or without a Pedestal, constitute the chief supporting members; the Frieze and Cornice, with the roof that rests upon them, constitute the chief part of the load they carry. The Architrave, the Arches, and the Spandrels form part of the load, relatively to what is below them, but are supporting members relatively to what is above them.

Besides being valuable as a shelter, a building may be in itself a noble and delightful object, and architects are builders who, by giving a building good proportions and fine details, and by employing beautiful materials, make it valuable on its own account, independently of its uses. Their chief instruments in this work are Drawings, both of the whole building and, on a larger scale, of the different features which compose it and of their details, which are often drawn full size. These drawings comprise Plans, Sections, Elevations, and Perspective Views, Fig. 15. They serve to explain the intention of the architects to their clients and to their workmen.

MOLDINGS—PLATE I

THE simplest decorative details and those that are most universally used in buildings are called *Moldings*. They are plane or cylindrical surfaces, convex, concave, or of double curvature, and they are sometimes plain and sometimes enriched by carving. They are called by various technical names: Greek, Latin, Italian, French, and English. The cross-section of a molding is called its *Profile*.

A small plane surface is called a *Band*, *Face*, or *Fascia*, Fig. 16, and if very small a *Fillet*, *Raised* or *Sunk*, Fig. 17, *Horizontal*, *Vertical*, or *Inclined*.

A convex molding is called an *Ovolo*, Fig. 18, *Torus*, Fig. 19, or *Three-quarter Molding*, Fig. 20, according to the amount of the curvature of its profile. A small Torus is called a *Bead*, Fig. 21, *Astragal*, or *Reed*, and an elliptical one, a *Thumb Molding*, Fig. 22. Concave moldings are, in like manner, called *Cavetto*, Fig. 23, *Scotia*, Fig. 24, or *Three-quarter Hollow*, but the term Scotia (darkness) is often used for any hollow molding. A Cavetto tangent to a plane surface is called a *Congé*, Fig. 25.

A molding with double curvature is called a *Cyma*, or Wave Molding. If the tangents to the curve at top and bottom are horizontal, as if the profile were cut from a horizontal wavy line, it is called a *Cyma Recta*, Fig. 26; if vertical, as if cut from a vertical line, a *Cyma Reversa*, Fig. 27. The Cyma Recta is sometimes called Cyma Reversa, Fig. 26 (*c*), when it is turned upside down. But this leads to confusion. The Cymas vary also, Fig. 28, in the shape and relative size of their concave and convex elements. A small Cyma is called a *Cymatium*. A small molding placed above a Band, or any larger molding, as a decoration, is also called a *Cymatium*, Fig. 29, whatever its shape.

When a convex and a concave molding, instead of being tangent, come together at an angle, they constitute a *Beak Molding*, Fig. 30.

Some architectural features, such as Bases, Caps, and Balusters, consist entirely of moldings. Others consist mainly of plane surfaces, moldings being employed to mark the boundary between different features, as between the Architrave and Frieze, or between different members of the

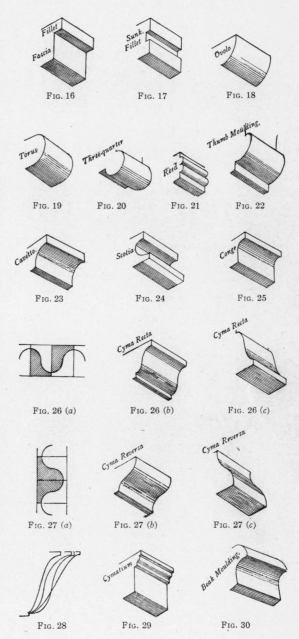

FIG. 16   FIG. 17   FIG. 18

FIG. 19   FIG. 20   FIG. 21   FIG. 22

FIG. 23   FIG. 24   FIG. 25

FIG. 26 (*a*)   FIG. 26 (*b*)   FIG. 26 (*c*)

FIG. 27 (*a*)   FIG. 27 (*b*)   FIG. 27 (*c*)

FIG. 28   FIG. 29   FIG. 30

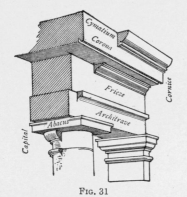

FIG. 31

FIG. 32

FIG 33

same feature, as between the Shaft of a column and its Capital, Fig. 31. In these cases the moldings, since they occur on the edges of the stone blocks, indicate, while they conceal, the position of the joints of the masonry. Moldings are often placed also in the internal angle where two plane surfaces meet, as is the case between the Frieze and the Corona of the Cornice, and under the Abacus of the Capital. When placed upon the external angle formed by two planes, they are, in the Gothic Styles, Fig. 32, often cut in, so as to lie below the surface of both planes, but in the Classical Styles, they project beyond the plane of one of the surfaces, like a little cornice, as is often seen in the Abacus of a Capital.

Horizontal Moldings, separating plane surfaces, are called a *String-Course*, Fig. 33.

TABLE OF MOLDINGS, PLATE I

Plane.—Face, Band, or Fascia; Beveled, Inclined, or Splay Face; Fillet, vertical, horizontal, or beveled, Raised or Sunk.

Convex.—Ovolo, or Quarter Round; Torus, or Half Round; Thumb Molding, or Elliptical Torus; Three-quarter Round; Bead, Astragal, or Reed; Three-quarter Bead.

Concave.—Cavetto or Quarter Hollow; Congé; Half Hollow; Scotia; Three-quarter Hollow.

Double Curvature.—Cyma Recta; Cyma Reversa; Cymatium; Beak Molding.

Besides the differences of size and shape already mentioned, and indicated in the table, moldings of the same name differ in the kind of curve they employ. They may be arcs, either of circles, ellipses, parabolas, or hyperbolas, or of any other curve

STYLES

DIFFERENT systems of construction have prevailed among different races, some employing only the Beam and Column, some also the Arch and Vault. In the choice of moldings, also, some have adopted one set of forms, some another. The forms employed by the Greeks and Romans constitute what are called the Classical Styles; those used in the Middle Ages, the Byzantine, Romanesque, and Gothic Styles. Some of the Gothic moldings have special names, such as Bowtel, Scroll, etc.

At the close of the Middle Ages, about four hundred years ago, the Classical styles were revived, as the Medieval styles have been during the last hundred years. Both are now in use. The styles of Egypt, India, and China are employed only occasionally and as a matter of curiosity.

THE ORDERS

In the Classical styles, several varieties of Column and Entablature are in use. These are called the *Orders*. Each Order, Fig. 34, comprises a Column with Base, Shaft, and Capital, with or without a Pedestal, with its Base, Die, and Cap, and is crowned by an Entablature, consisting of Architrave, Frieze, and Cornice. The Entablature is generally about one-fourth as high as the Column, and the Pedestal one-third, more or less.

The principal member of the Cornice is the Corona, Fig. 35. Above the Corona, the Cornice is regularly terminated by a member originally designed to serve as a gutter to receive the water running down the roof. It generally consists of a large Cyma Recta, though the Ovolo and the Cavetto are often used. It is called the *Cymatium*, in spite of its large size, and whatever its shape.

Note.—The word *Cymatium* thus has three meanings: (1) A small Cyma. (2) A small crowning member, of whatever shape, though it is most frequently a Cyma Reversa. (3) The upper member of a Cornice, occupying the place of a gutter, whatever its shape, though it is generally a large Cyma Recta. In Classical Architecture, the Cyma Recta seldom occurs, except at the top of the Cornice and at the bottom of the Pedestal.

It would seem as if a cornice that occurs at the top of a wall and carries the edge of a roof would properly have a Cymatium, this being the place for a gutter, and that Cornices used as String Courses, half way up a wall, would naturally be without this member. But the significance of the Cymatium has frequently been overlooked, in ancient times and in modern. Many Greek temples have a Cymatium on the sloping lines of the gable, where a gutter would be useless, Fig. 120, and none along the Eaves, and in many modern buildings the cornices are crowned by large Cymatia in places where there are no roofs behind them.

The Corona is supported by a Molding or group of Moldings, called the *Bed Mold*. A row of brackets, termed *Blocks*, Fig. 36, *Modillions*, or *Mutules*, Fig. 37, according to their shape, resting on the Bed Mold and supporting the soffit of the Corona, is often added. At the top of the Architrave is a projecting molding that, when square, is called a *Tænia*, and the face of the Architrave is often broken up into two or three Bands or Fascias, Fig. 38, each of which often carries a small molding as a Cymatium or covering member.

The Abacus of the Capital also has a sort of bed mold beneath it, which, when convex, is called an *Echinus*, Fig. 39, from the sea shell, Fig. 40, which it resembles in shape. The little Frieze below it is called the *Necking*. But if the

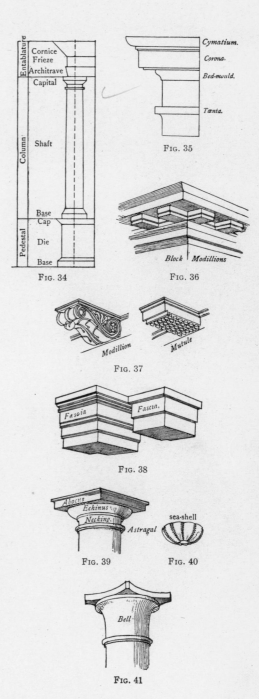

Fig. 34

Fig. 35

Fig. 36

Fig. 37

Fig. 38

Fig. 39   Fig. 40

Fig. 41

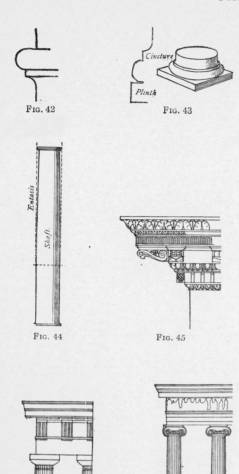

FIG. 42   FIG. 43

FIG. 44   FIG. 45

bed mold under the Abacus is concave, it dies into the necking like a large Congé, and the two together constitute the *Bell* of the Capital, Fig. 41. The Abacus is square in plan, but the Echinus, or the Bell below it, is round, like the column.

At the top of the shaft is a member called the *Astragal*, consisting of a Bead, Fillet, and Congé. It has a flat surface on top, as wide as the projection of the Congé, Fig. 42. At the bottom of the shaft is another Congé, called the *Apophyge*, below which is a broad fillet called the *Cincture*, Fig. 43. The Base generally has, below the base moldings, a plain member called the *Plinth*, which is square in plan like the Abacus.

The Shaft diminishes as it rises, Fig. 44, and the outline is not straight, but curved. This curve, which is called the *Entasis*, or bending, as of a bow, generally begins one-third of the way up, the lower third being cylindrical. The Entasis is not to be confounded with the *Diminution*, which is generally one-sixth, the upper Diameter being five-sixths of the lower.

The Pedestal also generally has a Corona and Bed Mold, but no gutter, and sometimes a Frieze, or Necking, above the Die, and a Base Molding and Plinth below it.

In the choice and use of moldings, the tastes and fashions of the Greeks and Romans were quite contrary to those of their successors in the Middle Ages. The Ancients preferred to use vertical and horizontal surfaces at right angles to each other, and seldom used an oblique line, or an acute or obtuse angle, as the Gothic architects did. They also preferred the Cyma Reversa, seldom employing the Cyma Recta, which in the Middle Ages was rather the favorite. Moreover, as has been said, the Gothic architects, in decorating a corner or edge, often cut it away to get a molding, but the Ancients raised the molding above the plane of the surface to which it was applied. In the composition and sequence of moldings also, the Classical architects generally avoid repetition, alternating large and small, plane and curved, convex and concave. The convex and concave profiles seldom describe an arc of more than 180 degrees, and except in the case of the Beak Molding and of the Bead, moldings are always separated by Fillets. When a molding is enriched, it is generally by carving ornamental forms, Fig. 45, upon it which resemble its own profile. The Greeks frequently employed elliptical and hyperbolic profiles, while the Romans generally used arcs of circles.

Among the Greeks, the forms, Fig. 46, used by the Doric race, which inhabited Greece itself and had colonies in Sicily and Italy, were much unlike those of the Ionic race, which inhabited the western coast of Asia Minor, and whose art was greatly influenced by that of Assyria and Persia. The Romans modified the *Ionic* and *Doric* styles, Fig. 47, and also devised a third, which was much more elaborate than

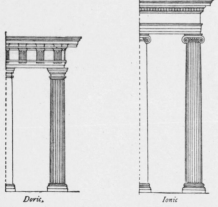

Doric   Ionic

FIG. 46.   Greek Orders

Doric.   Ionic

FIG. 47.   Roman Orders

either of them, and employed brackets, called *Modillions*, in the Cornice. This they called the *Corinthian*, Fig. 48. They used also a simpler Doric called the *Tuscan*, Fig. 49, and a cross between the Corinthian and Ionic called the *Composite*, Fig. 50. These are the *Five Orders*. The ancient examples vary much among themselves and differ in different places, and in modern times still further varieties are found in Italy, Spain, France, Germany, and England.

The best known and most admired forms for the Orders are those worked out by Giacomo Barozzi da Vignola, in the 16th century, from the study of ancient examples. The Orders that are shown in the large Plates almost exactly follow Vignola's rules.

Corinthian.
FIG. 48

Composite.
FIG. 50

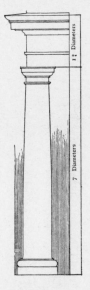

Tuscan
FIG. 49

VIGNOLA'S ORDERS—PLATE II

PLATE II shows the proportions of the Orders according to Vignola, in terms of the lower diameter of the columns. These vary in height from seven diameters to ten.

NOTE.—It is worth noting that, in ordinary handwriting, the T, for Tuscan, looks like a 7; D, for Doric, like an 8; I, for Ionic, like a 9; Co, for Corinthian and Composite reminds one of 10.

The Entablature is in all of them ordinarily one-fourth the height of the column, but it is sometimes made as small as one-fifth. The projection of the Cornice is the same as its height, except in the Doric Order, where it is greater. The lower band of the Architrave is made to come in line with the upper face of the shaft.

But it is only when seen in elevation that these relations obtain. When seen in perspective, as is generally the case, the cornice appears much larger, in proportion, and the frieze and architrave, being foreshortened, much smaller, and the architrave overhangs the shaft, Figs. 53 and 57.

In the Greek Orders, the Column is from five to ten diameters in height and the Entablature always about two diameters. In the Greek Orders, accordingly, the taller the Column, the lighter the Entablature, relatively; but in the Roman Orders, the taller the Column, the heavier the Entablature, actually. It follows that the weight of the Greek Entablature is proportioned to the diameter of the Column, irrespective of its height; of the Roman to the height of the Column, regardless of its diameter. The Romans put the least weight on the shortest and strongest supports. The Greek plan shows more regard to principles of construction, the Roman to principles of decorative composition.

Vignola used half of the lower diameter of the Column as his unit of measure, or *Module*. This he divided into twelve Parts for the Tuscan and Doric Orders, and into eighteen Minutes for the others, and he gives all the dimensions both of the larger members and of the moldings in terms of Modules and Parts, or Minutes, sometimes using even the quarter Minute, or one one-hundred-and-forty-fourth of a Diameter. But it is equally practicable and more convenient to use the whole *Diameter* as a unit of measure, dividing it only into Fourths and Sixths, and occasionally using an Eighth or a Twelfth.

In Plates IV, VI, VII, IX, XI, and XIII, the first column on the left shows the vertical dimensions as given in Plate II. In the second column, these divisions are subdivided into equal parts, the third column giving a further division of the dimensions thus obtained. Most of these dimensions can be stated in terms of sixths or fourths of the Diameter, as appears in the Tables. This analysis does not reach the smaller details, the shape and size of which must be learned by observation. Indeed, all these forms should be made so familiar that they can be drawn accurately from memory, these arithmetical relations being used only to test the accuracy of the result, or to discover how much the proportions adopted in any given case differ from the regular type. For Vignola's Orders are to be regarded only as an admirable standard that may be safely adopted when there is no occasion to do anything else, but which is to be departed from and varied whenever there is any reason for doing so. Vignola obviously so regarded them. He did not himself adhere closely to his own rules, or generally adopt his Orders in his own work. His Doric and Ionic are to be found, however, in the Villa Caprarola.

THE TUSCAN ORDER—PLATES III AND IV

THE distinguishing characteristics of the Tuscan Order is simplicity. Any forms of Pedestal, Column, and Entablature that show but few moldings, and those plain, are considered to be Tuscan. Such are, in antiquity, those of the Temple of Piety in Rome, Fig. 51, and the lower order of the Amphitheater at Arles. Vignola's Tuscan Order, Fig. 52, is marked by the use of the Ovolo in the Cymatium, and by the frequent employment of the Congé. The height of the Column is seven Diameters and that of the Entablature accordingly seven-quarters, or a Diameter and three-quarters. The Base, Capital, Architrave, and Frieze are each half a Diameter high, and the Cornice three-quarters. But this measurement includes not only the Base itself, but the Cincture at the foot of the Shaft. Dividing the Cornice into four parts, the Capitals into three, and the Base into two, gives the principal horizontal divisions. The Bed Mold is a large Cyma Reversa. The Abacus is seven-sixths of a Diameter across, not including the Fillet at the top, and it projects its own height from the face of the Architrave above, which is in line with the Necking below.

All the principal dimensions can be expressed in terms of fourths and sixths of the lower Diameter of the Shaft.

Vignola makes the width of the Plinth a little greater than this, and sets the Bed Mold up one-twelfth, making the Frieze wider and the Corona narrower.

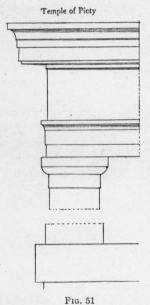

Temple of Piety

FIG. 51

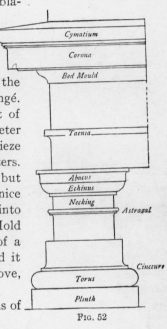

FIG. 52

TABLE OF THE TUSCAN ORDER—PLATES III AND IV

$\frac{1}{4} D$ equals height of Plinth.

$\frac{3}{4} D$ "   height of Cornice.

      "   projection of Cornice.

$\frac{1}{6} D$ "   height of Necking.

      "   height of Echinus.

      ·"   height of Abacus.

$\frac{1}{2} D = \frac{3}{6} D$ "   height of Base, including Cincture.

      "   height of Capital.

      "   height of Architrave.

      "   height of Frieze.

$\frac{5}{6} D$ "   upper Diameter of Shaft.

$\frac{6}{6} D$ "   lower Diameter of Shaft.

$\frac{7}{6} D$ "   width of Abacus.

$\frac{8}{6} D$ "   width of Plinth.

$\frac{1}{12} D$ "   width and projection of Tænia.

$\frac{1}{16} D$ "   height of Astragal and projection of Astragal.

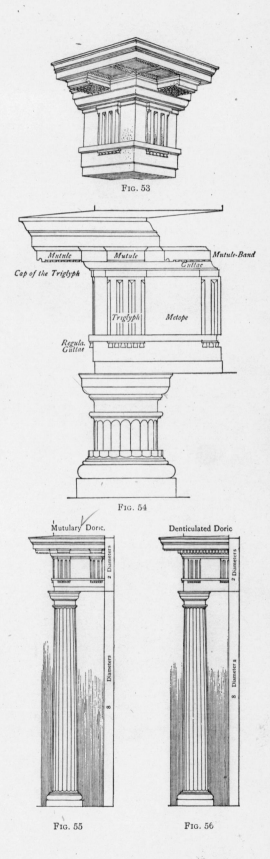

FIG. 53

FIG. 54

FIG. 55   FIG. 56

THE DORIC ORDER—PLATES V, VI, AND VII

THE distinguishing characteristics of the Doric Order, Figs. 53 and 54, are features in the Frieze and in the Bed Mold above it, called *Triglyphs* and *Mutules*, which are supposed to be derived from the ends of beams and rafters in a primitive wooden construction with large beams. Under each Triglyph, and beneath the Tænia that crowns the Architrave, is a little Fillet called the *Regula* or *Listel*. Under the Regula are six long drops, called *Guttæ*, which are sometimes conical, sometimes pyramidal. There are also either eighteen or thirty-six short cylindrical Guttæ under the soffit of each Mutule. The Guttæ are supposed to represent the heads of wooden pins, or treenails.

Two different Doric Orders are in use, the *Mutulary*, Figs. 53, 54, and 55, and the *Denticulated*, Figs. 56, 57, and 58. They differ chiefly in the cornices. In both of them the height, of three-quarters of a Diameter, is divided into four equal parts, the upper one embracing the gutter, or Cymatium, and the Fillet below, the next the Corona and the small Cyma Reversa, or Cymatium, above it. But the Bed Molds are unlike. In both of them, the lower member of the Bed Mold is a broad fillet, a sort of Upper Tænia, called the *Cap of the Triglyph*. This, unlike the Tænia below, breaks around the angles of the Triglyph, serving as a sort of crowning member, or cymatium, to both the Triglyph and the Metope.

In the Mutulary Doric, above the Cap of the Triglyph, is a narrow fillet that does not break around the angles and accordingly shows a broad soffit over the Metopes and at the corner of the building. These two fillets occupy the lower half of the lower quarter of the cornice. The upper half of the lower quarter, above this little fillet, is an Ovolo, and above this, the second quarter of the Cornice is occupied by a broad Fascia, called the *Mutule Band*, upon which are planted the *Mutules*, one over each Triglyph, which are half a Diameter wide, like the Triglyphs below them. They are broad, low, oblong brackets crowned with a Fillet and Cyma Reversa, which also crown the Mutule Band between the brackets. On the soffit of each Mutule are thirty-six Guttæ and a drip molding.

2

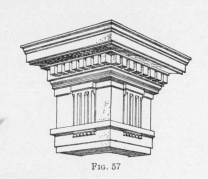

FIG. 57

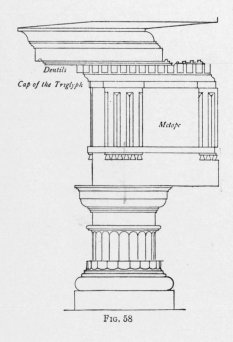

FIG. 58

In the Denticulated Doric, Figs. 56, 57, and 58, the place of the Fillet and Ovolo above the Cap of the Triglyph is taken by a large Cyma Reversa, the soffit of which is wider over the Metopes than over the Triglyphs, as is that of the small Fillet in the Mutulary. Above this molding is a band like the Mutule Band, but instead of brackets, extending out under the Corona, it bears a row of small blocks, like teeth called *Dentils*. These are one-eighth of a Diameter high, and are set one-eighth of a Diameter from center to center, or edge to edge. If this last dimension is divided into thirds, two of these go to the Dentil, and one to the space between it and the next one. This space is called an *Interdentil*, which is accordingly one twenty-fourth of a Diameter wide. The Dentil is thus one-eighth of a Diameter long and one-twelfth wide, or half a sixth, or of the proportions of two to three, like the Triglyph. The face of the last Dentil on the corner and the side of the first one around the corner come together in elevation without any Interdentil, giving the appearance of a *Double Dentil*, for the Dentils are square in plan and the side is just as wide as the face, Fig. 58.

As the Triglyphs are a Diameter and a quarter on centers, or ten-eighths, there are ten Dentils to each Triglyph and Metope.

A Dentil comes just over the axis of each Column and there are three Dentils between the one over the corner Column and the Double Dentil on the corner, the farther edge of the third one being just over the face of the Frieze, or five-twelfths of a Diameter from the axis of the Column.

The last Dentil, or first half of the Double Dentil, is centered over the outer face of the bottom of the shaft, Fig. 92.

The Dentils constitute the upper member of the Bed Mold. They leave the chief part of the Corona unsupported, but the soffit of the Corona, which is slightly inclined, recalling the slope of the rafters, is not so wide as the soffit of the Mutulary Doric, owing to this encroachment of the Dentils. The Mutules, which are very shallow, have, accordingly, only eighteen Guttæ in place of thirty-six; that is, three rows instead of six. There is also a Mutule over each Metope, as well as one over each Triglyph.

Vignola gives his Denticulated Doric a large Cavetto for a Cymatium, or gutter, instead of a Cyma Recta, and supports the Echinus of the Capital by three fillets, instead of by a Fillet and Bead, Fig. 58.

The Triglyphs are three-quarters of a Diameter high and half a Diameter wide, Fig. 59. This width is divided into three parts, called *Shanks*. Each Shank, or *Femur*, is beveled on the edge nearly up to the top of the Triglyph, making in all two channels and two half channels. Each Shank is one-sixth of a Diameter wide and each beveled face a quarter of a sixth. The plain face of the Shank is, accordingly, one-twelfth, and just as wide as the channel. These are almost the only beveled faces to be found in the whole range of Classical Architecture, though beveled fillets are not uncommon. The two full channels are generally cut in at an angle of 45 degrees, but the two half channels on either side are shallower, and do not reach the face of the Frieze.

A Triglyph comes exactly over each Column, and one or two over each Intercolumniation. The portion of the Frieze between the Triglyphs is called a *Metope*. It is exactly square, being three-quarters of a Diameter wide. The fragment of a Metope between the last Triglyph and the corner of the Frieze is one-sixth of a Diameter wide. The face of the Metopes comes over the lower band of the Architrave, and that of the Triglyph projects slightly beyond the face of the upper Band.

The Column is eight Diameters in height, the Base, Capital, and Architrave each half a Diameter, the Frieze and Cornice each three-quarters. The total projection of the Cornice, including the Cymatium, is one Diameter. The Architrave is divided into two Bands, or Fascias. The lower one occupies the lower third of the Architrave, and the Tænia, Regula, and Guttæ the upper third. Half of this third goes to the Tænia, the projection of which equals its height.

The Doric Column has twenty *Channels*, each about one-sixth of a Diameter wide, which show in section, Fig. 60, an arc of 60 degrees. The solid edge that separates them, called the *Arris*, makes an angle of something over 90 degrees (102 degrees). The ten Arrises shown in elevation are easy to draw, as two come on the outline of the Shaft, two come on its "corners," and the two middle ones are almost exactly one-sixth of a Diameter apart. The channels are .157 of a Diameter wide, so that making the middle one-sixth, or .166 of a Diameter, involves an error of only .009 of a Diameter, or about one-eighteenth of its width. The four other Arrises can then be put in without much difficulty.

The Doric Base and Capital, Figs. 54 and 58, are divided, like the Tuscan, into halves and thirds, but with additional moldings, a bead being added above the Torus of the Base, and another below the Echinus of the Capital. The Abacus is crowned by a cymatium consisting of a Fillet and Cyma Reversa. If the height of the Capital is divided into thirds, each of the two upper thirds again into thirds, and the upper and lower of these still again into three equal parts, all the horizontal lines of the Capital will be determined, as shown in Plate V. The base, including the Cincture, as in the Tuscan Order, is half a Diameter high.

Vignola's Denticulated Doric is imitated closely from the Doric Order of the Theater of Marcellus, and the Mutulary, which he has been thought to have invented, seems to have been derived from the Doric Order of the Basilica Julia, Fig. 61. There are no Roman Doric temples.

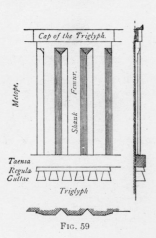

FIG. 59

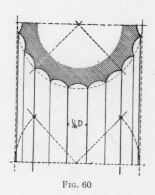

FIG. 60

Cornice of the Basilica Julia.

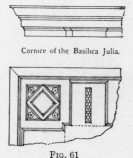

FIG. 61

TABLE OF THE DORIC ORDER—PLATES V, VI, AND VII

$\frac{3}{4} D$ equals height of Frieze.
  " height of Cornice.
  " projection of Corona (Denticulated).
  " projection of Mutule (Mutulary).
  " width of Metope.

$\frac{1}{4} D$ " height of Plinth.
$\frac{1}{6} D$ " projection of Plinth.
  " projection of Abacus.
  " height of Abacus.
  " height of Necking.
  " height of Echinus and Bead.
  " height of Lower Band.
  " height of Guttæ, Regula, and Tænia.
  " width of Shank.
  " width of Corner Metope.

$\frac{1}{2} D = \frac{3}{6} D$ " height of Base, including the Cincture.
  " height of Capital.
  " height of Architrave.
  " width of Triglyph.

$\frac{1}{8} D$ " height of Dentils.
  " distance of Dentils o. c.
$\frac{1}{12} D$ " width of Dentils.
  " height of Tænia.
  " projection of Tænia.

$\frac{1}{16} D$ " height of Astragal.
  " projection of Astragal.

$\frac{1}{24} D$ " width of Interdentils.

THE IONIC ORDER—PLATES VIII AND IX

THE prototypes of the Ionic Order are to be found in Persia, Assyria, Fig. 62, and Asia Minor. Like the Doric Order, it seems to have been imitated from a wooden construction. It is characterized by Bands in the Architrave and Dentils in the Bed Mold, both of which are held to represent sticks laid together to form a beam or a roof. But the most conspicuous and distinctive feature is the *Scrolls* that decorate the Capital of the Column. These have no structural significance, and are purely decorative forms derived from Assyria and Egypt. Originally the Ionic Order had no Frieze and no Echinus in the Capital. These were borrowed from the Doric Order, and, in like manner, the Dentils and Bands in the Doric were imitated from the Ionic. The Ionic Frieze was introduced in order to afford a place for sculpture, and was called by the Greeks the *Zoöphorus*, or Figure Bearer, Fig. 64.

In the Ionic Entablature, the Architrave, Frieze, and Cornice are about the same height, each measuring about three-quarters of a Diameter. But Vignola makes the Architrave a little smaller and the Cornice a little larger, so that they measure, respectively, five-eighths, six-eighths, and seven-eighths of a Diameter. The Architrave is divided into five parts, each an eighth of a Diameter in height. The upper one is occupied by a large Cyma Reversa and Fillet, which take the place of the Doric Tænia. Below are two fascias, or bands, of equal height, each measuring a quarter of a Diameter. The lower one is crowned by an Ovolo and Fillet. The French often use three bands, as in the Corinthian Architrave.

The Ionic Frieze is plain, except for the sculpture upon it. It sometimes has a curved outline, as if ready to be carved, and is then said to be *Pulvinated*, from *Pulvinar*, a bolster, which it much resembles.

The Cornice is much like that of the Denticulated Doric, which was derived from it, but has no Mutules. The upper half, as in the Doric, is taken up by the Cymatium and Corona, and the lower half by the Bed Mold.

This is divided into four equal parts, of which the upper one is given to an Ovolo, the lower to a Cyma Reversa and Fillet, and the two middle ones to a Dentil Band and Fillet. Upon this band are planted the Dentils, which are one-sixth

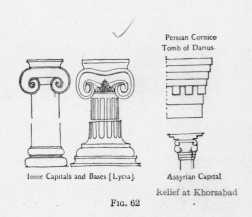

Ionic Capitals and Bases [Lycia]. Assyrian Capital.

Persian Cornice Tomb of Darius.

Relief at Khorsabad

FIG. 62

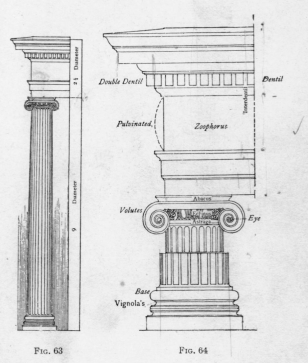

FIG. 63　　　　　　　　FIG. 64

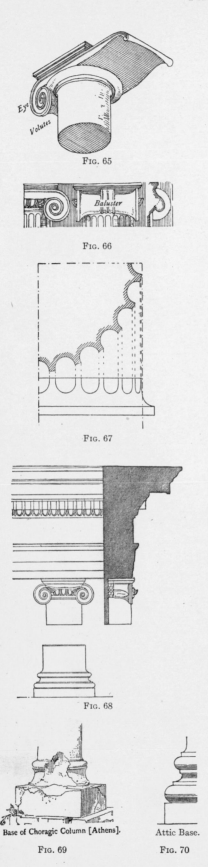

FIG. 65

FIG. 66

FIG. 67

FIG. 68

Base of Choragic Column [Athens].

FIG. 69

Attic Base.

FIG. 70

of a Diameter high, and are set one-sixth on centers, or on edges, instead of one-eighth, as in the Denticulated Doric. Two-thirds of this sixth go to the width of the Dentil and one to the space between, or Interdentil. The Dentil is, accordingly, one-ninth of a Diameter wide, and the Interdentil one-eighteenth, instead of a twelfth and a twenty-fourth. A Dentil is put on the axis of a column, and an Interdentil comes just over the outer line of the Frieze. There is, apparently, a Double Dentil on the corner, the outer face of which is two-thirds of a Diameter, or four-sixths, from the axis of the column. The first half of it, as in the Denticulated Doric, comes over the outer face of the lower end of the shaft, Fig. 93. There are two Dentils between the one over the column and the Double Dentil, in place of three, as in the Doric.

The Ionic Capital, like the Doric, has an Echinus and an Abacus crowned by a Cyma Reversa and Fillet. But generally it has no Necking, and it is, accordingly, only two-sixths of a Diameter in height, or one-third instead of one-half. Both the Echinus and the Cymatium that crowns the Abacus are larger than in the Doric, and the face of the Abacus smaller, and the Echinus projects in front of the Abacus, instead of being covered by it. The Abacus and its Fillet extend beyond the Echinus on either side, and are curled up into the Scrolls, or *Volutes*, Fig. 65, the whole height of which is a half Diameter, measuring down from the Architrave. The *Eyes* of the Scrolls are one-third of a Diameter from the top, on the line separating the bottom of the Capital from the top of the Astragal that crowns the Shaft. They are just one Diameter apart on centers, coming over the outer lines of the lower end of the Shaft, and the inner edges of the Scrolls are two-thirds apart. The Echinus is generally carved with Eggs and Darts, three of which show between the Scrolls, the next one on either side being hidden by sprigs of Honeysuckle Ornament. These Scrolls, Fig. 66, show on the sides a series of moldings called the *Baluster*, or *Bolster*. The term Abacus is generally held to apply only to the Cyma Reversa and Fillet, above the Scrolls.

The Shaft of the column is ornamented with twenty-four *Flutings*, Fig. 67, semicircular in section, which are separated not by an Arris, but by a Fillet of about one-fourth their width. This makes the Flutings only about two-thirds as wide as the Doric Channels, or about one-ninth of a Diameter, instead of one-sixth. Four-fifths of one twenty-fourth of the circumference is .106 of a Diameter, while one-ninth of the Diameter is .111, a difference of less than a twentieth.

The typical Ionic base is considered to consist mainly of a Scotia, as in some Greek examples, Fig. 69. It is common, however, to use instead what is called the *Attic Base*, Fig. 70, consisting of a Scotia and two Fillets between two large Toruses, mounted on a Plinth, the whole half a Diameter high. The Plinth occupies the lower third, or one-sixth of a Diameter. Vignola adopted for his Ionic Order a modification of the Attic Base, substituting for the single large Scotia two small ones, separated by one or two Beads and Fillets and omitting the lower Torus, Fig. 64.

The principal ancient examples of the Ionic Order in Rome are those of the Theater of Marcellus, Fig. 71, and of the Temple of Fortuna Virilis, Fig. 72.

The Ionic Capital sometimes has a necking like the Doric, which is then generally decorated, Fig. 73. Sometimes, also, the four faces of the Capital are made alike, double scrolls occurring at the corners, where they project at an angle of 45 degrees. In this case there is no Baluster, and the Capital resembles the upper portion of a Composite Capital. It is then sometimes called the Roman Ionic Capital, or the Scamozzi Capital, Fig. 74, from the name of the architect, Scamozzi, who frequently employed it.

Almost all the dimensions of the Ionic Order can be expressed in terms of sixths of a Diameter, as appears in the following Table:

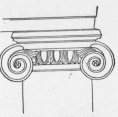

Theatre of Marcellus

FIG. 71

Temple of Fortuna Virilis

FIG. 72

Scamozzi Capital

FIG. 74

Roman Capital [in the Lateran Museum].

FIG. 73

TABLE OF THE IONIC ORDER—PLATES VIII AND IX

$\frac{5}{8} D$ equals height of Architrave.

$\frac{3}{4} D = \frac{6}{8} D$ " height of Frieze.

$\frac{7}{8} D$ " height of Cornice.

" projection of Cornice.

$\frac{1}{4} D = \frac{2}{8} D$ " height of each Band.

$\frac{1}{6} D$ " projection of Plinth.

" height of Plinth.

" height of Dentils.

" distance of Dentils, o. c.

" projection of Abacus.

$\frac{1}{3} D = \frac{2}{6} D$ " height of Capital.

$\frac{1}{2} D = \frac{3}{6} D$ " height of Base.

" height of Scrolls.

$\frac{2}{3} D = \frac{4}{6} D$ " distance between Scrolls.

" distance from Axis to outer face of Double Dentil.

$\frac{5}{6} D$ " upper Diameter.

$1 D = \frac{6}{6} D$ " lower Diameter.

" distance of Eyes of Scrolls, o. c.

" length of Baluster.

$\frac{7}{6} D$ " width of Abacus.

$1\frac{1}{3} D = \frac{8}{6} D$ " width of Plinth.

" width of Echinus (minus).

$1\frac{1}{2} D = \frac{9}{6} D$ " width of Scrolls (minus).

$\frac{1}{9} D$ " width of Dentil.

" width of Fluting.

$\frac{1}{12} D$ " height of Astragal.

" projection of Astragal.

$\frac{1}{18} D$ " width of Interdentil.

THE CORINTHIAN ORDER—PLATES X AND XI

THE three distinguishing characteristics of the Corinthian Order, Fig. 75, are a tall bell-shaped Capital, a series of small brackets, called *Modillions*, that support the Cornice instead of Mutules, in addition to the Dentils, and a general richness of detail, which is enhanced by the use of the *Acanthus leaf*, Fig. 76, in both Capitals and Modillions.

The Cornice, Fig. 77, which is one Diameter in height, is divided into five equal parts. The two lower and the two upper parts resemble the lower and upper halves of the Ionic Cornice. The middle fifth is occupied by a *Modillion Band*, which carries the Modillions, or brackets. These, as well as the Modillion band, are crowned by a small Cyma Reversa. They consist of a double scroll, beneath which is an Acanthus leaf. Each Modillion is five-twelfths of a Diameter long; i. e., half the upper Diameter of the Shaft, one-fifth high, and is as wide as a Dentil and two Interdentils; that is to say, two-ninths of a Diameter. It is about square in the front elevation, and about two squares in the side elevation and in plan. They are set two-thirds of a Diameter on centers, one being over the axis of the corner Column, and one over the outer face of the Double Dentil. The interval between them is four-ninths of a Diameter, or just twice their width. The soffit of the Corona between the Modillions is occupied by a sinkage with moldings, called a *Caisson*, in the middle of which there is a large *Rosette*.

As the Modillions are two-thirds of a Diameter on centers, or four-sixths, and the Dentils are one-sixth, on centers, it follows that there are four Dentils to each Modillion; i. e., a Dentil under every Modillion, and three between. As in the Ionic Order and in the Denticulated Doric, the last Dentil, which is the first half of the Double Dentil, is centered over the face of the lower Diameter of the column, Fig. 94.

But these dimensions and proportions vary greatly in different ancient examples and almost as much in modern ones. The Architrave, which is three-quarters of a Diameter high, has three Bands and a large cymatium, which is as wide as the first Band. The two lower Bands occupy the lower half of the Architrave, and the third Band and the cymatium the upper. A small Bead, or a small Cyma Reversa, generally crowns each Band. The Frieze, which is also three-quarters of a Diameter high, may be plain, pulvinated, or sculptured.

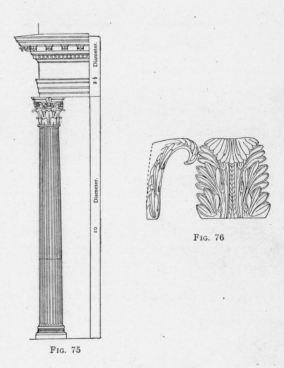

FIG. 75

FIG. 76

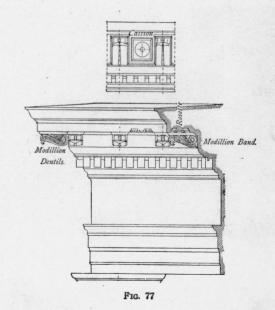

FIG. 77

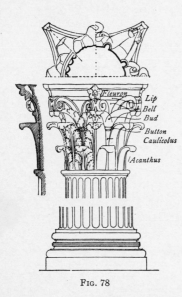

FIG. 78

FIG. 79

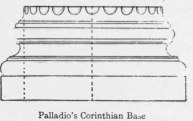

Palladio's Corinthian Base

FIG. 80

The Capital, Fig. 78, is seven-sixths of a Diameter high, the upper sixth being taken up by the Abacus, which is nine-sixths, or a Diameter and a half, in width, though it does not look so. It is molded on the edge with an Ovolo and Fillet above a large Congé and small Fascia. The corners are cut off at an angle of 45 degrees, and the sides hollowed out in a curve of 60 degrees. The width across from curve to curve is seven-sixths of a Diameter. Each face of the Abacus bears a flower, called the *Fleuron*, that springs from a small bud above the middle leaf.

The *Bell* of the capital, Fig. 79, is one Diameter high, or six-sixths; it terminates under the Abacus in a Beak Molding called the *Lip of the Bell* which measures seven-sixths of a Diameter across, its greatest projection coming just under the least projection of the upper line of the Abacus. The lower two-sixths are covered by a row of eight Acanthus leaves, which bend down at the top to the extent of half a sixth, or a quarter of their own height. The next two-sixths show a similar row of eight leaves, set alternately with those below, four facing the sides of the Capital, and four the corners. Like those of the first row, they spring from the Astragal at the top of the Shaft, and the mid-rib of each leaf shows between two lower leaves, it being really four-sixths high. These also bend down half a sixth. Between the eight leaves of the second row are eight *Caulicoli*, or cabbage stalks, which terminate in a *Button*, upon which rests a sort of *Bud*, which divides into two leaves. These turn right and left, the larger one toward the corner of the Capital, the smaller toward the side or front under the Fleuron. From each Bud rise also two scrolls, or Volutes, one of which runs out to support the projecting corner of the Abacus. The other, which is smaller, and does not rise higher than the Lip of the Bell, supports the Fleuron. The sixteen leaves of the third row curl over under these sixteen volutes, making with them eight masses of ornament, one on each corner of the column, and one in the middle of each side. These give in plan an eight-pointed star, each point consisting of a large leaf, two small leaves, two Volutes, and above them, either the Fleuron or the horn of the Abacus. Between them is seen the Bell of the Cap, with its Lip.

Here, again, the Attic Base is commonly used, but sometimes, especially in large columns, a base is used that resembles Vignola's Ionic Base, with two Beads between the Scotias, except that it has a lower Torus, Fig. 78. Palladio uses a very elegant variety of Attic Base, enriched by the addition of Beads and Fillets, Fig. 80. The Shaft is fluted like the Ionic shaft, with twenty-four semicircular flutings, but these are sometimes filled with a convex molding, or *Cable*, to a third of their height, Fig. 75.

Almost all the buildings erected by the Romans employ the Corinthian Order.

TABLE OF THE CORINTHIAN ORDER—PLATES X AND XI

$\frac{3}{4} D$ equals height of Architrave.
     " height of Frieze.

$1 D = \frac{4}{4} D$ " height of Cornice.
     " projection of Cornice.

$\frac{1}{6} D$ " projection of Plinth.
     " height of Plinth.
     " height of Lower Band.
     " height of Dentils.
     " distance of Dentils, o. c.

$\frac{1}{3} D = \frac{2}{6} D$ " height of Leaves.
     " projection of Abacus.

$\frac{1}{2} D = \frac{3}{6} D$ " length of Modillion, including Cymatium.

$\frac{2}{3} D = \frac{4}{6} D$ " distance of Modillions, o. c.
     " distance from Axis to face of Double Dentil.

$\frac{5}{6} D$ " upper Diameter.

$1 D = \frac{6}{6} D$ " lower Diameter.
     " height of Bell.
     " height of Cornice.
     " projection of Cornice.

$\frac{7}{6} D$ " height of Capital.
     " width of Abacus (least).
     " width of Lip of the Bell.

$1\frac{1}{3} D = \frac{8}{6} D$ " width of Plinth.
$1\frac{1}{2} D = \frac{9}{6} D$ " width of Abacus (greatest).
$2 D = \frac{12}{6} D$ " width of Abacus (diagonal).
$\frac{4}{9} D$ " width of Caisson.
$\frac{1}{9} D$ " width of Dentil.
$\frac{2}{9} D$ " width of Modillion, excluding Cymatium.
$\frac{4}{9} D$ " length of Modillion, excluding Cymatium.
     " distance between Modillions.
$\frac{1}{18} D$ " width of Interdentil.
$\frac{1}{12} D$ " height of Astragal.
     " projection of Astragal.
$\frac{5}{12} D$ " length of Modillion.
$\frac{1}{6} D$ " height of Modillion, including Cymatium.

THE COMPOSITE ORDER—PLATES XII AND XIII

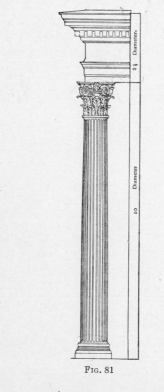

FIG. 81

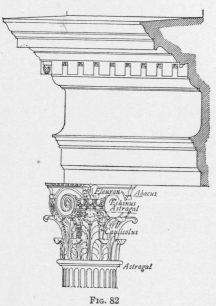

FIG. 82

THE Composite Order, Fig. 81, is a heavier Corinthian, just as the Tuscan is a simplified Doric. The chief proportions are the same as in the Corinthian Order, but the details are fewer and larger. It owes its name to the Capital, Fig. 82, in which the two lower rows of leaves and the Caulicoli are the same as in the Corinthian. But the Caulicoli carry only a stunted leaf-bud, and the upper row of leaves and the sixteen Volutes are replaced by the large Scrolls, Echinus, and Astragal of a complete Ionic Capital, with four faces like Scamozzi's. A Composite Capital thus has two Astragals, if the lower be included, but this properly belongs to the shaft. The Scrolls are nearly half a Diameter high, covering up half the Abacus and coming down so as to touch the second row of Acanthus leaves. They measure fully nine-sixths across, and are only three-sixths apart, or half a Diameter, instead of four-sixths, as in the Ionic.

Vignola's Composite Entablature, Fig. 82, differs from his Ionic chiefly in the shape and size of the Dentils. They are larger, and are more nearly square in elevation, being a fifth of a Diameter high, and one-sixth wide, the Interdentil being one-twelfth, and they are set one-fourth of a Diameter apart, on centers. The last Dentil, or first half of the Double Dentil, is centered over the outer face of the Column, at the bottom, as in the Corinthian, Ionic, and Denticulated Doric, Fig. 95. The outer face of the Double Dentil is three-quarters of a Diameter from the axis of the Column, and there is only one Dentil between the Double Dentil and the one over the axis, against two in the Corinthian and Ionic, and three in the Denticulated Doric. The Frieze terminates in a large Congé over the Architrave, and the Corona is undercut with a large quirked Cyma Recta, making a drip.

Palladio's Composite Entablature, Fig. 83, has more characteristic than Vignola's, the parts being fewer and larger. The Architrave has two Bands, the Frieze terminates in two large Congés, and the Cornice is divided into two equal parts, each half a Diameter high. The upper half is shared about equally by the Cymatium and the Corona, and the lower half is almost entirely taken up by a series of large brackets, or *Blocks*, a third of a Diameter high, and one-fourth wide, divided into two Bands. The inner face of the *Double Block* comes just in line with the Frieze below, Fig. 102. The bands and moldings that decorate the Blocks are continued between them.

These dimensions apply to Palladio's entablature where it is made of the same size as Vignola's, that is to say, a quarter of the height of the column, or two Diameters and a half. But Palladio himself made his Composite entablature only two Diameters high, or one-fifth of the length of the column, cutting down the Frieze to half a Diameter, the Architrave to two-thirds, and the Cornice to five-sixths. If the dimensions of Palladio's Cornice given in the table are, accordingly, taken from the upper diameter of the shaft instead of from the lower, they will exactly conform to Palladio's own usage.

The Block entablature used by Scamozzi for his Composite Order is even less than two Diameters in height, and this seems to have been the case also with the entablature of the Olympiæum at Athens, which Palladio is thought to have imitated.

The moldings below the Blocks are often made to project more than in Palladio's example. This increases their distance apart, on centers, since one must still come over the axis of the column and the one on the corner must be as far out as the end of these moldings. The Blocks also vary considerably in length in different examples.

The upper part of the Composite Capital, as has been said was used alone by Scamozzi and others as a variety of the Ionic Capital, Fig. 74.

The Composite Capital is employed in the Arch of Titus in Rome, and elsewhere, with a Corinthian entablature, and the Block Cornice occurs in the so-called frontispiece of Nero, as well as in the temple at Athens, in connection with a Corinthian Capital.

FIG. 83

TABLE OF THE COMPOSITE ORDER—PLATES XII AND XIII

$\frac{1}{2}D = \frac{3}{6}D$ equals height of Scrolls.
         "   space between Scrolls.

$\frac{3}{4}D$ "   distance of Eyes, o. c.

$1\frac{1}{2}D = \frac{9}{6}D$ "   width of Scrolls.
         "   width of Plinth.
         "   width of Abacus.

VIGNOLA'S CORNICE

$\frac{1}{4}D$ "   height of Dentil Band.
         "   distance of Dentils, o. c.

$\frac{3}{4}D$ "   distance from Axis to face of Double Dentil.
$\frac{1}{5}D$ "   height of Dentils.
$\frac{1}{6}D$ "   width of Dentils.
$\frac{1}{12}D$ "   width of Interdentil.

PALLADIO'S CORNICE

$\frac{1}{3}D$ "   height of Block.
         "   length of Block.

$\frac{1}{4}D$ "   width of Block.
         "   height of Lower Band.
         "   height of Corona.
         "   height of Cymatium.
         "   distance between Blocks (*plus*).

GEOMETRICAL RELATIONS

THE dimensions and proportions set forth in the previous paragraphs, and recapitulated in the Tables, enable one to draw the Five Orders, according to Vignola, with great accuracy and sufficiently in detail for all the ordinary purposes of the draftsman and designer. The figures for the larger features are easily remembered, and the smaller divisions and subdivisions can for the most part be obtained by dividing the larger into two, three, four, or five equal parts.

But besides these arithmetical proportions some geometrical relations may be pointed out, which are calculated greatly to facilitate the work of draftsmanship, drawing being naturally more closely related to Geometry than to Arithmetic.

LINES AT 45 DEGREES

The proportions of any figure that is as wide as it is high, and which can accordingly be included within a square, are most easily determined by drawing the diagonal of the square, that is to say, by drawing a line with a 45-degree triangle. Such figures are, as is shown in the Illustrations, the projections of:

1. The Echinus, in the Tuscan, Doric, and Ionic Capitals, Figs. 84 and 85.

2. The Abacus, in the Tuscan and Doric Capitals, Figs. 84 and 85.

3. The Astragal, in all the Orders, Fig. 86.

4. The Architrave, including the Tænia, in the Tuscan and Doric Orders, counting from the axis of the Column, Figs. 84 and 85.

5. The Tænia itself, and the Cymatium that takes its place, Figs. 84 and 85.

6. All the Cornices, except the Doric, Fig. 84.

A line drawn at 45 degrees through the Doric Cornice from the top of the Frieze gives, where it cuts the upper line of the Cornice:

7. The face of the Corona, in the Denticulated Doric, Fig. 85.

8. The face of the Mutule, in the Mutulary Doric, Fig. 85.

A line drawn at 45 degrees through the Doric Architrave and Frieze, from a point on the axis of the Column and of the Triglyph, taken either at the bottom of the Architrave or at the top of the Frieze, gives:

9. The Axis of the next Triglyph, and so on, Fig. 85.

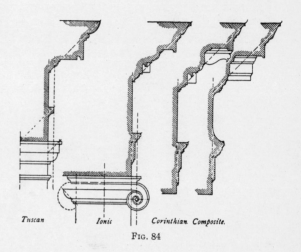

Tuscan   Ionic   Corinthian. Composite.

FIG. 84

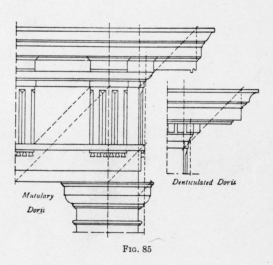

Denticulated Doric

Mutulary Doric

FIG. 85

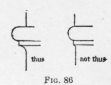

thus   not thus

FIG. 86

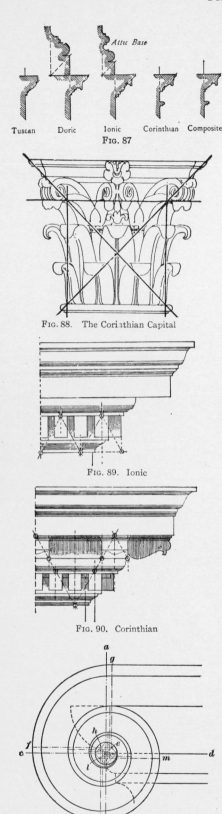

Tuscan　Doric　Ionic　Corinthian　Composite
FIG. 87

FIG. 88.　The Corinthian Capital

FIG. 89.　Ionic

FIG. 90.　Corinthian

FIG. 91.　The Ionic Capital

A 45-degree line also gives:

10.　The Shape of the Metope, Fig. 85.

11.　The Caps of the Pedestals, except the Tuscan, Fig. 87.

12.　The Plinths of the Doric and Attic Bases, Fig. 87.

Lines drawn at an angle of 45 degrees across the Corinthian Capital from the extremities of its lower diameter give:

13.　The width of the Abacus, Fig. 88.

Where they cut the line of the upper diameter of the shaft, extended, they give:

14.　The depth of the Scroll, Fig. 88.

LINES AT 60 DEGREES

In like manner, lines drawn at an angle of 60 degrees through the Bed Mold of the Ionic Cornice from a point on the axis of the Column, taken either on the upper line of the Frieze or on the upper edge of the Dentil Band, give, where they touch the upper line of the Frieze and the upper line of the Dentil Band:

15.　The Axes of the Dentils, and the outer face of the Double Dentil, Fig. 89.

Similar lines drawn at 60 degrees in the Corinthian Cornice, taken from a point where the axis of the Column cuts the lower edge of the Corona, give:

(a)　Where they cut the lower edge of the Corona, the upper line of the Frieze, and the lower line of the Ovolo:

16.　The Axes of the Modillions and of the Dentils, and the outer face of the Double Dentil, very nearly, Fig. 90.

(b)　Where they cut the lower line of the Modillion Band:

17.　The width of the Modillion, and the outer face of the Modillion Band, Fig. 90.

(The distance from the edge of the Corona down to the lower edge of the Modillion Band is one-third the distance down to the top of the Frieze, and the distance down to the lower edge of the Ovolo, one-half.)

THE IONIC VOLUTE

The vertical line $a\,b$, Fig. 91, through the center of the eye of the Ionic Volute, and the horizontal line $c\,d$, will mark in the circumference of the eye the four corners of a square within which a fret may be drawn whose angles will serve as centers, from which the curves of the volute may be described mechanically. The sides of the square above referred to should be bisected, and through the upper points thus located a horizontal line $e\,f$ should be drawn. Now, with $e\,g$ as a radius, the arc $g\,f$ may be drawn as the first section of the volute. Now, through the point h, where the line $e\,f$ bisects the side of the square, a vertical line $h\,k$ should be drawn, and with $h\,f$ as a radius the arc $f\,k$ may be struck. From h and e lines should be drawn at 45 degrees, intersecting at the center of the eye, and the line extending from *h* to the center should be divided into three equal parts, through which the corners of the inscribed fret will turn. The point *l* on the line *h k*, marking the lower left-hand corner of the inscribed fret, is located five-sixths of the distance between *h* and the point where *h k* bisects the lower side of the square. *l* then forms the center for the arc *k m*, and the rest of the volute is described from centers found at the angles of the inscribed fret.

VERTICAL LINES

The outer line of the upper Diameter of the Shaft gives, in all the Orders, Figs. 84 and 85:

18. The face of the lower band of the Architrave, and
19. The face of the Frieze.

In the Denticulated Doric, it gives, Fig. 85:
20. The outer face of the first Dentil, next the Double Dentil.

In the Ionic and Corinthian Orders, it gives, Figs. 84 and 85:
21. The axis of the first Interdentil.

The outer line of the lower Diameter of the Shaft, produced upwards, gives, Figs. 84 and 85:
22. The projection of the Astragal, in all the Orders, except the Tuscan and Doric.
23. The projection of the Tænia in the Tuscan and Doric.
24. The projection of the Fillet, in the Bed Mold of the Mutulary Doric, Fig. 85.
25. Twice the projection of the Triglyph which is seen in profile.
26. Half the projection of the Tuscan Bed Mold, of the Tuscan and Doric Abacus, and of the Doric Mutule Band.

It also gives:
27. The Axis of the Extreme Dentil, or of the first half of the Double Dentil, in the Denticulated Doric, Ionic, Corinthian, and Composite Orders, Figs. 92, 93, 94, and 95.
28. The position of the Eye of the Ionic Scroll, which is on a level with the bottom of the Echinus, Fig. 91.

FIG. 92.　Doric

FIG. 93.　Ionic

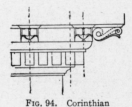

FIG. 94.　Corinthian

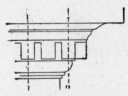

FIG. 95.　Composite

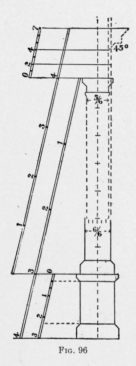

Fig. 96

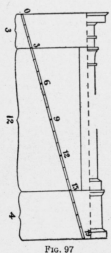

Fig. 97

DRAWING

General Proportions.—Since the relative size of all the parts, in Vignola's Orders, is fixed, any of them can be drawn out in accordance with these rules, if a single dimension is determined. The width of a Dentil or the length of a Modillion suffices to determine everything else. But the data generally given are either the lower Diameter of a Column, the height of a Column, or the whole height of the Order, with or without a Pedestal.

I. If the lower Diameter is given, the procedure is as follows, Fig. 96: Divide it in two, draw the axis of the Column, and then divide each half into three equal parts, Fig. 109; this gives the scale of sixths. Divide in two the two outer sixths; this gives the upper Diameter of the shaft, which is five-sixths. Lay off on the axis the height of the Column—by Diameters, 7, 8, 9, or 10—and of the Entablature, which is one-fourth the height of the Column. Mark the height of the Base, half a Diameter, or three-sixths, and then that of the Capital, two-, three-, or seven-sixths.

Then divide the total height of the Entablature into seven, eight, eighteen, or ten equal parts, according as it is Tuscan, Doric, Ionic, or Corinthian, or use halves, quarters, or eighths of a Diameter, and mark the heights of the Architrave, Frieze, and Cornice, drawing horizontal lines through the points of division. (Fig. 96 illustrates this procedure for the Tuscan Order.) Then carry up, vertically, the outer lines of both the upper and the lower Diameters of the Shaft, drawing from the point where the line of the upper Diameter cuts the lower edge of the Cornice a line at 45 degrees to determine the projection of the Cymatium, or, in the Doric Orders, that of the Mutule or of the Corona.

Add one-third of the height of the Column for the Pedestal. Divide this into three equal parts, taking the upper third of the upper third for the Cap, and the lower two-thirds of the lower third for the Base, Fig. 96. Vignola makes the Base of the Pedestal only one-ninth of the height of the Pedestal instead of two-ninths as here determined.

II. If the height of the Column is given, a fourth part of this added at the top gives the height of the Entablature, and a third part added below gives the height of the Pedestal, Fig. 96. One seventh, eighth, ninth, or tenth of the height of the Column gives the lower Diameter of the Shaft. The drawing may then be carried forwards as above.

III. If the total height of the Order is given, without the Pedestal, a division into five equal parts gives four parts for the Column and one for the Entablature, Fig. 96.

If there is a Pedestal, and it is of the regular height of one-third the height of the Column, the division of the total height must be into nineteen equal parts, four of which go to the Pedestal, twelve to the Column, and three to the Entablature, Fig. 97.

The lower Diameter can then be obtained from the height of the Column, and the drawing completed, as above.

NOTE.—The division of a given dimension into equal parts may be effected with the dividers, or, more easily, by using a scale of equal parts that are the same in number as the desired subdivisions, but a little larger, and holding this scale obliquely between the extreme limits of the space to be divided, Figs. 96 and 97. The division of vertical dimensions into five, seven, eight, nine, ten, eighteen, or nineteen equal parts, as here required, is thus easily accomplished. To insure accuracy, the lines marking these divisions should be horizontal, not normal to the direction of the scale.

Cornices.—The Tuscan Cornice may be drawn by dividing its height into quarters, as is done in the figure, giving the upper quarter to the Ovolo and the lower to the bed mold, and the middle half to the Corona, Bead, and Fillet, Fig. 98. A 45-degree line gives the projection of the Bed Mold, Ovolo, and the Cornice itself.

The Doric Cornice is also divided into four equal parts, the upper one comprising the Cymatium and Fillet, the next the Corona and the small Cyma Reversa above it, the third the Mutules (or the Dentils with the Mutules above them), and the lower one the Bed Mold, including the Cap of the Triglyph, which is narrower in the Mutulary Doric than in the Denticulated by the width of the Fillet above it, Figs. 99 and 100.

A 45-degree line drawn outwards from the middle of the top of the Abacus gives, where it cuts the lower line of the Frieze, the projection of the Tænia. A similar line, where it cuts the upper line of the Frieze, gives the axes of the next Triglyph, Fig. 85. The Triglyphs are drawn next, with their Cap, and the Regula and Guttæ, then the Mutules, or the Dentils.

In the Doric Order a line at 45 degrees drawn from the bottom of the Cornice gives the face of the Corona in the Denticulated Doric, the face of the Mutule in the Mutulary; in the other Orders, a similar line gives the projection of the Cymatium, Figs. 99 and 100.

In putting in Dentils, draw first the one over the Axis of the Column, then the Double Dentil, the first half of which is centered over the lower face of the Column, and then the intermediate ones, three, two, or one, according as the Order is Doric, Ionic, Corinthian, or Composite, Figs. 92, 93, 94, and 95. The Interdentil is half the width of the Dentil.

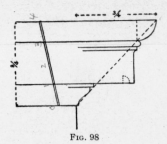

FIG. 98

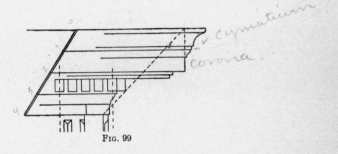

FIG. 99

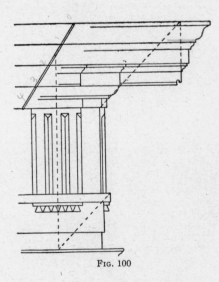

FIG. 100

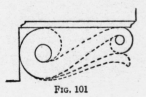

FIG. 101

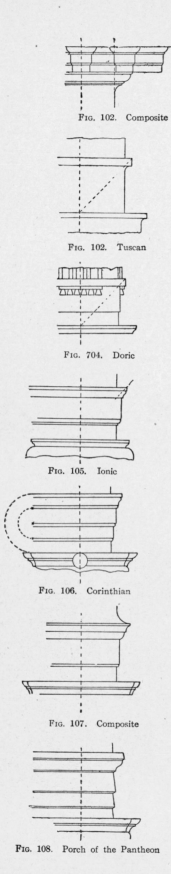

FIG. 102.   Composite

FIG. 102.   Tuscan

FIG. 704.   Doric

FIG. 105.   Ionic

FIG. 106.   Corinthian

FIG. 107.   Composite

FIG. 108.   Porch of the Pantheon

One Corinthian Modillion comes over the axis of the corner column and one over the outer face of the Double Dentil, Fig. 94. In drawing the side of a Modillion, put in first, at the outer end, a semicircle half its height and one at the inner end nearly the whole height; then the rosettes, one twice as large as the other; then the connecting curves, and finally the leaf beneath, Fig. 101.

In Palladio's Composite Cornice, one block is set over the axis of the column, and the double block at the corner has its inner face on a line with the face of the Frieze below. The blocks are about half a Diameter, on centers, the inter-block being one twenty-fourth of a Diameter wider than the block itself, Fig. 102.

Architraves.—The Tuscan Architrave, Fig. 103, has but one fascia or band, the Composite two, Fig. 107, and the Corinthian three, Fig. 106. The Doric has sometimes one, but generally two, Fig. 104, and the Ionic has generally two, Fig. 105, but sometimes three. The lower band is always the narrowest and is set on a line with the face of the Shaft below and of the Frieze above.

All the Architraves have a Cymatium, or crowning member, which in the Tuscan and Doric is a broad Fillet, called the Tænia, and in the Ionic and Corinthian is a large Cyma Reversa, surmounted by a Fillet and generally supported by a bead. The lower bands often have, as a Cymatium, a small Cyma Reversa, Bead, or Ovolo, and all three bands are sometimes sloped backwards, as in the Entablature of the porch of the Pantheon in Rome, Fig. 108, so as to diminish the projection of the crowning moldings, which otherwise have a projection, beyond the face of the Frieze, equal to their height.

The Tuscan Tænia has beneath it the characteristic Tuscan congé, Fig. 103. Beneath the Doric Tænia, and directly under each Triglyph, Fig. 104, is a narrow Fillet, which sometimes has a beveled face, called the Regula, beneath which are the six Guttæ. These are sometimes frusta of cones, as in the Greek Order, sometimes of pyramids. The Guttæ, which almost touch at the bottom, are twice as high as the Regula. Both together are just as high as the Tænia, or one-twelfth of a Diameter, so that the three are one-sixth of a Diameter high. They accordingly occupy the upper third of the height of the Architrave, which is three-sixths high, the lower band occupying the lower third.

The two lower bands of the Corinthian Architrave occupy half its height, and the lower band with its Cymatium is just as wide as the moldings that crown the upper band. The second band with its Cymatium is just as wide as the third band without its Cymatium, Fig. 106.

Capitals and Bases.—In drawing Capitals, it is best to put in first the axis of the column and the vertical faces of the Shaft; then the horizontal lines, and lastly the profile, beginning at the top. But in drawing Bases, it is best to put in the profile of the molding before the horizontal lines.

The Tuscan Base, Fig. 109, is half a Diameter high, half of which goes to the Plinth and half to the Base Molding, which is made to include the Cincture, or broad Fillet at the bottom of the Shaft, counted as part of the Base. The same is true of the Doric Base. But this is merely saying that the Tuscan and Doric Bases are not quite half a Diameter high.

All the other Bases, including the Attic Base, are just half a Diameter high. All the Plinths are eight-sixths wide and one-sixth high, except the Tuscan and Doric, which are one-quarter of a Diameter high.

The Tuscan Capital, Fig. 109, is half a Diameter high, or three-sixths, the upper sixth comprising the Abacus with its Fillet, the middle sixth the Echinus and the Fillet below it, and the lower sixth the Necking. The upper Fillet is a quarter of a sixth wide, the lower one a sixth of a sixth. The Abacus is seven-sixths wide; i. e., it projects one-sixth on each side beyond the upper diameter of the Shaft.

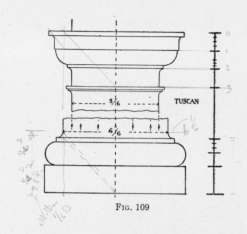

FIG. 109

The Doric Capital, Fig. 110, is also three-sixths of a Diameter high, the two upper sixths being divided into thirds, and these again into thirds, to give the height of the smaller moldings. The Denticulated Capital generally has three Fillets, the Mutulary, a Bead and Fillet.

The Astragal, which in the other Capitals is one-twelfth of a Diameter high, or half a sixth, is in the Tuscan and Doric Orders one-fourth smaller, or one-sixteenth of a Diameter, the Bead being one twenty-fourth of a Diameter high, or a quarter of a sixth. In drawing the Astragals, draw first the horizontal line at the top, which occupies two-thirds of the projection, otherwise the Congé below is apt to be slighted. The Bead and Congé should have their full measure of 180 degrees and 90 degrees, Fig. 111.

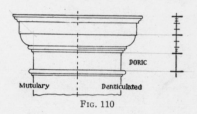

FIG. 110

The Ionic Capital, which is one-third of a Diameter in height, or four-twelfths, is also divided into three parts, but unequally. The Abacus occupies the upper quarter, or one-twelfth, and had better be put in first. The Echinus occupies rather more than half of the remaining space, namely, five-ninths. In the Composite Capital, the Abacus occupies the upper sixth, and a little more, and the Echinus and the Astragal the next one, Fig. 82.

The Eyes of the Ionic Scroll come in line with the top of the Astragal and with the lower Diameter of the Column, and should be put in first, Fig. 112. The Scrolls make three complete turns and finally are tangent to the upper side of the eye. They can best be drawn by putting in first three semicircles on the outer side, and then three smaller ones on the inner side. In working on a small scale, two semicircles on each side suffice, or three on the outer side and two on the inner, as in the figures. But one is never enough. The Eyes of the Composite and of the Roman Ionic Capitals are set nearer together, Fig. 82.

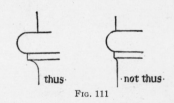

FIG. 111

In drawing a Corinthian Capital, Fig. 113, it is best to put

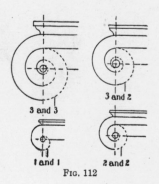

FIG. 112

4

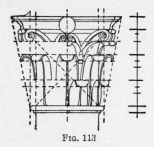

FIG. 113

FIG. 114

in first the Astragal and the lower line of the Architrave, carrying up on each side the outer lines of the Shaft; then the Abacus, Fleuron, and Scrolls. The double scroll at the corner falls just outside these vertical lines. It appears slightly elliptical in shape, not circular, and the outer scroll is more elliptical than the inner, being more foreshortened. The small scrolls under the Fleuron are also foreshortened into ellipses. Then the five leaves of second row, the middle one in elevation, the two side ones in profile, and the other two at 45 degrees, carrying down the mid-ribs to the Astragal. Their tips turn down half a sixth, those of the corner leaves coming just on the outer lines of the upper shaft. Of the four leaves of the lower row, the two inner ones occupy the spaces between these mid-ribs, and the ends that turn over fall entirely within the outline of the lower parts. The two outer leaves extend on either side slightly beyond the width of the shaft below, and their tips fall just outside the lower line of the leaves, being about six-sixths of a Diameter apart. They accordingly come just over the outer lines of the lower Diameter, just as the tips of the corner leaves above them come on the lines of the upper Diameter.

A line drawn tangent to the Astragal and to the Abacus is also tangent to all three rows of leaves, very nearly. The Caulicoli, the Buttons, the third row of leaves, and the lower parts of the Volutes follow, in this order.

The smaller the scale of the drawing, the more straight and upright should the Acanthus leaves be made, Fig. 114.

THE GREEK ORDERS

ALTHOUGH the different examples of the Greek Doric and Ionic Orders differ considerably among themselves, both in the proportions of the Columns and in the treatment of details, the proportions of the Entablature are tolerably uniform and are, in general, the same for both Orders, the Architrave and Frieze being both about three-quarters of a Diameter in height and the Cornice about half a Diameter, Figs. 115 and 122. The Entablatures, as has been said, are about two Diameters high, however tall or short the Columns may be. Their chief characteristic is the height of the Architrave and the shallowness of the Cornice. The Diminution and the Entasis of the Columns begin at the bottom of the Shaft.

THE GREEK DORIC—PLATE XIV

The Greek Doric has no Base, the Shaft standing upon three large steps, the upper one of which is called the *Stylobate*, Fig. 115. It has generally twenty channels, Fig. 116, which are generally elliptical in section, but some small Columns have only sixteen, or even, as at Argos, fourteen, Fig. 117. In a number of examples, an Arris instead of a Channel comes on the axis of the Column, as is seen both at Argos, Fig. 117, and at Assos, Fig. 118. Instead of an Astragal, a groove, or *Sinkage*, separates the Shaft from the Necking of the Capital, and the Channels are carried past it, through the Necking, quite up to the Fillets at the base of the Echinus, Fig. 116. These Fillets vary in number. They are not vertical on the face, but are parallel to the slope of the Echinus, and their upper surfaces also are beveled, Fig. 119. The Echinus itself has an elliptical or hyperbolic profile, the earlier examples being the most convex and the later ones hardly differing from a straight line. The Abacus has no moldings.

The Architrave also is plain, and is crowned by a Tænia, below which is a broad Regula and six short Guttæ. In the earlier examples, the face of the Architrave is set just over and in line with the upper Diameter of the Shaft, but in the later ones it overhangs, coming over the lower Diameter, and the Echinus is made straighter, as has been said, and steeper, as if to support it.

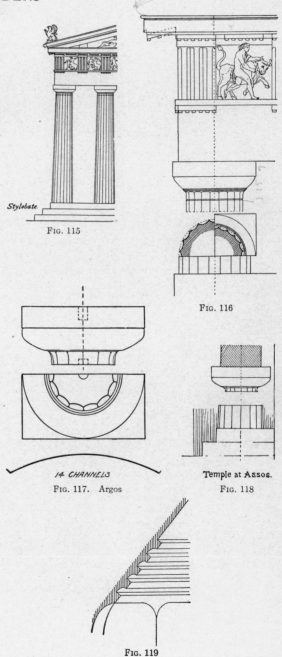

Stylobate.

FIG. 115

FIG. 116

14 CHANNELS
FIG. 117. Argos

Temple at Assos.
FIG. 118

FIG. 119

FIG. 120

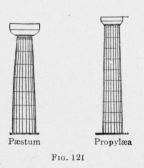

Pæstum   Propylæa

FIG. 121

The Triglyphs in the Frieze are shorter and broader than in the Roman Doric, and are set flush with the Architrave below, the Metopes being set back. They are also thicker than those in the Roman Orders, and the channels are much larger, being one-fourth wider,—measuring two-ninths, or four-eighteenths, of the width of the Triglyph instead of one-sixth, or three-eighteenths,—and also deeper. The half channels on the edges go back at an angle of 45 degrees, and the two whole channels generally at 60 degrees, the cross-section being thus an equilateral triangle cutting deeply into the face of the Triglyph; they run nearly up to the broad Fillet, or Band, that constitutes the Cap of the Triglyph. This is only as wide as the Triglyph itself, not breaking round the corners, and it is not continued between the Triglyphs, the Cap of the Metopes being narrower.

As in Vignola's Denticulated Doric, the Mutules on the Soffit of the Corona slope up, and have only eighteen Guttæ, and they occur over the Metopes as well as over the Triglyphs, Fig. 120. The Mutules are thicker than those in the Denticulated Doric, though not so thick as in the Mutulary. The Cymatium generally consists of an elliptical Ovolo and a Fillet, the Soffit of which is beveled. But different examples vary in almost every one of these particulars.

At the corner of a building the Triglyphs are set, not over the axis of the Column, but at the extreme end of the Frieze, two coming together and making a solid block. As the Metopes do not vary in size, being nearly square, this brings the three corner columns nearer together than the others.

In the best Greek examples the axes of the columns all slope in a little, so that the corner column, which is a little bigger than the others, has its inner face nearly vertical. The horizontal lines, both of the Entablature and of the Stylobate, curve slightly, being convex up, the vertical faces incline a little, either out or in, and the moldings are, as has been said, generally elliptical or hyperbolic in section, rather than arcs of circles.

The columns vary in height from about five to eight Diameters, the earlier ones being the shortest, and the Entasis, or Curvature in the outline of the Shaft, and the Diminution in the width of the Shaft, from bottom to top, which sometimes amounts to one-third of the Diameter, are much more pronounced in the earlier examples than in the later ones, Fig. 121. This seems to show that the original of the Doric column was not a wooden post, as has been thought, nor a pile of masonry, but was probably a piece of rubble work, covered, like the rubble walls, with stucco.

THE GREEK IONIC—PLATE XV

THE general proportions of the Greek Ionic Entablature are, as has been said, about the same as in the Doric, but the Columns are more slender, varying from about seven Diameters in height to more than ten, and the Architrave, Frieze, and Cornice are often made very nearly equal in height, Fig. 122.

The Base is like the Attic Base, except that the Scotia is larger, constituting the principal feature, that the upper Torus is larger than the lower one, that the Fillet above the Scotia projects as far as the face of this Torus, and that there is no Plinth. As the base is still half a Diameter high, the upper Torus and Scotia are very much larger than in the Roman Attic Base. The lower Torus is sometimes very small indeed, and is occasionally omitted altogether, as at Samos, Fig. 123, and in one of the Choragic columns on the south side of the Acropolis at Athens, Fig. 69.

The Shaft is fluted just as in the Roman Ionic, having twenty-four channels, and the Capital resembles, in general, Vignola's Capital with Balusters. But the Scrolls are much larger, measuring a full Diameter and a half from side to side, and two-thirds of a Diameter from the Architrave to the bottom of the curve. The Capital, measured from the Architrave down to the Astragal, is half a Diameter high, instead of a third, the Abacus is very small, consisting generally of a single Ovolo, and the *Cushion* between the Abacus and the Echinus very wide, its lower outline being curved downwards, Fig. 124. The sprigs of honeysuckle, accordingly, do not cover the eggs and darts, five of which are visible between the Scrolls, instead of three.

The Architrave is sometimes plain, sometimes divided into two or three bands. The Frieze, or Zoöphorus, is wide, and the Bed Mold that crowns it is often countersunk into the Soffit of the Corona, so that it does not show in elevation, Fig. 122. It is noticeable that though Dentils are, historically, a distinctively Ionic feature, they are omitted in many Greek examples. The Cymatium is a large Cyma Recta, and has a Fillet and Bead below it, which is sometimes undercut, so as to make a little Beak Molding.

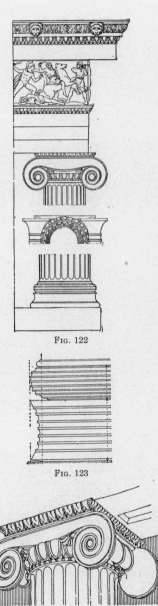

FIG. 122

FIG. 123

FIG. 124

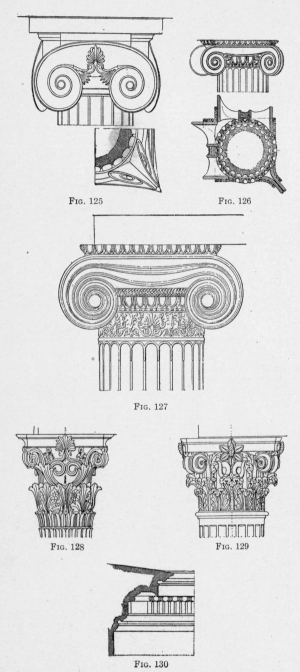

FIG. 125   FIG. 126

FIG. 127

FIG. 128   FIG. 129

FIG. 130

But here, as in the Greek Doric, there is a great variety in the details of different buildings.

The four faces of the Capital are sometimes made alike, with double Scrolls on each corner, as in Scamozzi's Ionic, and these Scrolls are sometimes connected under the Abacus by a continuous curve, convex up, instead of by a horizontal line, Fig. 125. Sometimes a corner column shows Scrolls on the two outer faces and Balusters on the two inner ones, the double scroll on the corner projecting at 45 degrees, Fig. 126. Some examples have a wide Necking, adorned with the honeysuckle ornament, below the Echinus, Fig. 127.

A few Corinthian Capitals are to be found in Greece, but the buildings in which they occur are in other respects Ionic, or even Doric, Fig. 128.

In the later Greek colonies in Southern Italy are found interesting varieties of all the Orders.

Their most marked peculiarity is the treatment of the details, Fig. 130. The Triglyphs and Dentils are long and slender, and the moldings refined in outline and sometimes separated by deep grooves, rectangular or circular, which are not to be mistaken for moldings. The Architraves lose their importance, the Ionic Scrolls are often diminished in size, and the egg-and-dart molding is changed into what are sometimes called *Filberts*, Fig. 131. The Corinthian Capitals receive a local development quite unlike that which was finally adopted in Rome itself, as may be witnessed at Tivoli, Fig. 129, Pompeii, and Herculaneum, Fig. 132. Since the revival of classical architecture other variations have appeared in France, Germany, and Italy.

FIG. 131   FIG. 132

PILASTERS—PLATE XVI

THE Romans made their Pilaster Capitals resemble those of the Columns. This works well, except with the Ionic Capital, in which the projecting Echinus presents an almost insuperable difficulty, Fig. 133.

As Pilasters do not generally diminish in width at the top, their Capitals are one-fifth broader than those of the Columns. If, in this case, the Architrave comes in line with the upper face of the column, the face of the Pilaster projects one-twelfth of a Diameter beyond it, as appears in the perspectives given in Plates III, IV, VIII, X, and XII. But Pilasters are often made half a sixth narrower than the Columns at the bottom, and half a sixth wider at the top, having thus a uniform Diameter of five-sixths and a half. In this case the base moldings are spread so as to make the plinth of the usual size, and in the Corinthian Pilaster Capital, the upper row of leaves, the volutes, and the abacus have the same dimensions as those of the columns, while the leaves of the two lower rows are made broader, Fig. 134.

Pilasters generally project from the wall a quarter of their diameter, but sometimes have to be made thicker in order to receive string-courses or other horizontal moldings that they cut across. If made much thicker than this, they are apt to look thicker than the columns alongside them, and piers always do, noticeably enhancing the slenderness of the columns near them.

Pilasters are generally plain, but if Ionic and Corinthian Pilasters do not diminish at the top they are often fluted. Since the columns have twenty-four channels and twenty-four fillets, and the diameter is nearly a third of the circumference, there is space on the Pilaster for eight channels and eight fillets, very nearly. But as the number of channels must be one less than the number of fillets, only seven are employed, with eight fillets. This has the advantage of putting a channel on the axis, and of making the two outer fillets wider than the others. It is common to omit the fluting on the sides. But a projection of a quarter of a Diameter gives room for one channel, and half a Diameter for three.

The Greeks gave their Pilasters Bases like those of the Columns, but Capitals of their own, composed of a series of moldings, Fig. 135.

Pilasters are preferable to half columns, which always look smaller than they are, and have a mean appearance. Moreover, any moldings that they interrupt seem to cut them in two, Fig. 136. In these respects, three-quarter columns are better, though they are apt to look clumsy, and they inevitably make an awkward junction with the wall behind them, especially if they are fluted. They also make it uncertain which is the principal supporting member, the wall or the column.

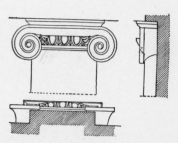

FIG. 133

FIG. 134

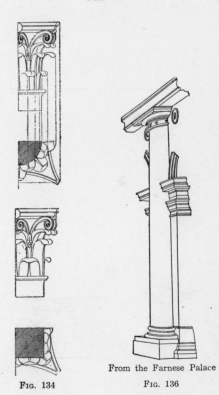

From the Farnese Palace

FIG. 136

FIG. 135

PEDESTALS—PLATE XVI

As has already been said, a short Pier is called a Post, and, if it supports something, a Pedestal, and the Pedestals that support Columns are generally made one-third the height of the Column. The Cap is one-ninth the height of the Pedestal, and generally consists of a Bed Mold and Corona. There is no Cymatium, a gutter being obviously out of place, but the Corona is often crowned by a fillet and small Cyma Reversa. The Base, which is two-ninths of the height of the Pedestal, or, according to Vignola, only one-ninth, like the Cap, consists of a Plinth and Base Moldings, among which a Cyma Recta is generally conspicuous, with a Torus below it.

The moldings, in both Cap and Base, are fewer and consequently larger and simpler in the Tuscan and Doric Orders than in the Ionic and Corinthian, the Tuscan, according to Vignola, having no Corona, and the Corinthian a Necking and Astragal. The Cap projects less than its own height, in many examples, and the Plinth just as much as the Corona.

But Pedestals vary greatly both in their proportions and in their moldings.

PARAPETS

A wall low enough to lean upon is called a *Parapet*, and whether low or high is often strengthened by occasional Posts or Pedestals, sometimes of the same height, sometimes higher. In either case the wall or parapet has a Cap and Base, which may or may not be like those of the Pedestals or Posts. A similar strip of wall, with the wall continued above the Cap, is called a *Continuous Pedestal*, Fig. 143. This often occurs between the Pedestals that support Pilasters.

BALUSTRADES

In antiquity, Parapets were often pierced by triangular penetrations, apparently in imitation of wooden fences, Fig. 137. But in modern times the openings in Parapets are generally filled with a sort of colonnade of dwarfed columns called *Balusters*. These frequently occupy the whole space between one Post or Pedestal and the next, forming a *Balustrade*, Fig. 138. If the distance is great, so that the Cap has to be made of several lengths of stone, a block called an *Uncut Baluster* is placed under the joint. Not more than a dozen Balusters should occur together without such interruption. Against the Pedestal is often set a *Half-Baluster*, or, which is better, half of an Uncut Baluster, to support the end of the Upper Rail, Fig. 139.

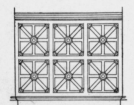

F<small>IG</small>. 137

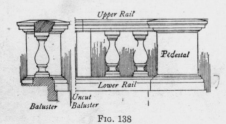

F<small>IG</small>. 138

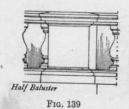

F<small>IG</small>. 139

The Cap and Base of the Pedestals, or of the Parapet or Continuous Pedestal, are called in a Balustrade the *Upper* and *Lower Rails*. The Baluster supports the Upper Rail as a Column supports an Entablature, and stands upon the Lower Rail as upon a Stylobate, Fig. 139. It has its own Cap, the height of which, including the Astragal, is one-quarter the height of the Baluster, and consists of a plain Abacus, Echinus and Fillet, and Necking. These three members are of about equal height, as in the Tuscan and Doric Capitals

The Base of the Baluster is also one-quarter its total height and resembles the Attic Base. The Scotia, as in the Greek Attic Base, is generally made the principal member.

Between the Cap and Base is the Shaft, or *Sleeve*, which has the outline of a Quirked Cyma Reversa, the greatest diameter, or *Belly*, coming at about one-fourth of its height, or one-third the height of the Baluster, Fig. 140. Its width at this point is also one-third the height of the Baluster, as is also that of the Plinth of the Base, exactly, and the width of the Abacus, almost. The Necking is less than half as wide. The point of contrary flexure in the Cyma Reversa is half way between Cap and Base, or between the Upper and Lower Rails. But these proportions are made somewhat lighter for use with the Ionic and Corinthian Orders.

The Rails are sometimes, in height, one-sixth and two-sixths of the space between them, like the Cap and Base of a Continuous Pedestal; but they are often made much heavier, even one-third and one-half.

Instead of the Cyma Reversa, a Beak Molding is often used, Fig. 141, and other variations are frequent. Of these, the most important is the so-called *Double Baluster*, which consists of two small Balusters, set together base to base just like the Baluster on the side of an Ionic Capital, Fig. 142. Vignola also used a high block under the Plinth. Balusters are often made square in section, like piers, instead of round, like columns.

Balusters are set about half their height apart, on centers.

A Balustrade, like a Parapet, is intended to lean upon, and should not be more than 3 or 4 feet high. While, therefore, Columns and Entablatures are proportioned to the size of the buildings in which they occur, varying in height from 10 or 12 feet to 50 or 60, Balustrades, like steps, are proportioned to the size of the human figure, and in large buildings are relatively much smaller than in small ones. They thus serve, as do steps, and as does the human figure when introduced into a drawing, to indicate the scale of a building.

But in very large buildings Balustrades have sometimes been made of colossal dimensions, that on the top of the front of St. Peter's, for example, being about 8 feet high.

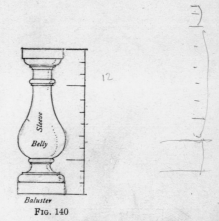

Baluster
FIG. 140

FIG. 141

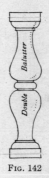

FIG. 142

Fig. 143

Fig. 144

ATTICS

When a Parapet is placed on top of an Entablature it is called an *Attic*, that is to say, an "Athenian" story, Fig. 143. Like Pedestals, Attics vary much in size and in architectural treatment. They are generally made about a quarter as high as the Order below, and should not be more than a third, and they should have a high Plinth, or even a double Plinth, Figs. 144 and 153, so as not to be too much hidden by the projection of the Cornices on which they stand.

The place of an Attic is often taken by Balustrades, Fig. 145, which also should have high Plinths, below the lower rail.

Fig. 145

PEDIMENTS—PLATE XVII

THE Gable upon a Classical building is called a *Pediment*, Fig. 146. It consists of a Triangular piece of wall, called the *Tympanum*, which is in the same plane as the Frieze below; of a *Horizontal Cornice*, which divides the Tympanum from the Frieze; and of two pieces of inclined cornice that surmount the Tympanum. The inclined, or *Raking, Cornice* is like the cornice that crowns the wall on the sides of the building, but the Cymatium is a little wider. The Horizontal Cornice has no Cymatium, and generally terminates in a Fillet, called the *Split Fillet*, which divides at the angle where the two Cornices come together.

If the Cymatium is a Cavetto, the under side of the Fillet beneath it is beveled, either on the rake or along the wall; if it is an Ovolo, the same thing happens to the Fillet above it, Fig. 147. With the Cyma Reversa both occur, with the Cyma Recta, neither, the fillets having no soffit. This is one of the reasons for employing this molding in this place.

When a Cyma Recta is used in the Cymatium, it occurs in four different forms, Fig. 148; viz.: (1) the profile of the molding along the wall; (2) the profile of the raking molding; (3) the line of intersection of these two moldings—this lies in a vertical plane, set at 45 degrees; (4) the line of intersection of the two raking moldings at the top. (1), (2), and (4) have the same projection but different heights; (1) and (3) have the same height but not the same projection.

According to Vignola, the obtuse angle at the top of the Pediment is included within an arc of 90 degrees. It accordingly has a slope of $22\frac{1}{2}$ degrees. This is a good rule for most cases. But if a building is high and narrow, the slope needs to be steeper, and if it is low and wide, flatter. Inasmuch, however, as, for a building of a given width, the higher it is, the larger is the scale of the Order employed and of all the details of the Order, it follows that, for a given width of front, the larger the moldings are, the steeper must be the slope.

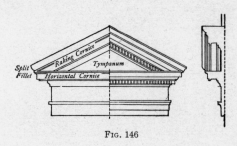

FIG. 146

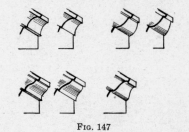

FIG. 147

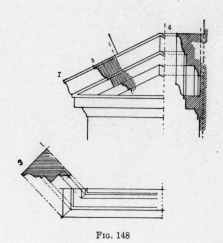

FIG. 148

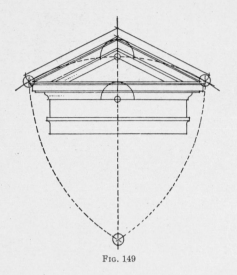

FIG. 149

Upon this is founded the following rule for the slope of Pediments, devised by Stanislas L'Eveillé, Fig. 149: Taking the upper line of the Horizontal Cornice as one side, construct below it an equilateral triangle, and taking the vertex of this triangle as a center, and its side as a radius, describe an arc of 60 degrees. Taking, then, the summit of this arc as a center, describe a circle, the radius of which is equal to the width of the horizontal cornice. Lines drawn from the extremities of the Corona tangent to this circle will give the upper line of the Raking Corona. It is obvious that the larger the cornice, relatively to the length of the front, the steeper will be the slope. It is also plain that this rule gives steeper Pediments for the Corinthian and Ionic Orders than for the Doric and Tuscan, and for the Roman Orders than for the Greek, the cornices being wider.

Circular, or *Curved, Pediments* have a sweep of 90 degrees, Fig. 150, starting at an angle of 45 degrees.

When Pediments are used merely for ornament the upper part is sometimes omitted, giving a *Broken Pediment*, Fig. 152.

If the molding that crowns the Corona is omitted, the faces of the three Coronas are continuous, Fig. 151. This was exemplified in Antiquity by the recently discovered Treasury of the Cnidians at Delphi.

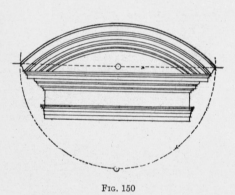

FIG. 150

FIG. 151

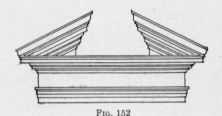

FIG. 152

In a Raking Cornice the modillions, dentils and egg-and-darts have their axes vertical and in line with those in the Horizontal Cornice beneath. But in the Maison Carrée at Nimes they are set at right angles with the Corona, and this is regularly done with the Eggs-and-Darts where an ovolo occurs alone, without dentils or modillions. If a modillion occurs at the apex of the pediment it is broken. This occurs when the center intercolumniation is Diastyle, with the columns four Diameters, or twelve thirds, on centers, giving five modillions over the opening between them, or with any other spacing which makes their distance on centers a multiple of four-thirds of a Diameter.

INTERCOLUMNIATION, OR THE SPACING OF COLUMNS—PLATE XVIII

THE space between two columns, measured just above their bases, is called an *Intercolumniation*. It is one Diameter less than their distance apart on centers, or on edges.

Columns are said to be *Coupled*, or to have a *Pycnostyle, Systyle, Diastyle,* or *Areostyle Intercolumniation,* according as they are set close together, or are one, two, three, or four Diameters apart, as nearly as may be; i. e., about one, two, three, four, or five Diameters on centers. The Systyle and Diastyle are the most usual, with an Intercolumniation of two or of three Diameters.

But Coupled Columns cannot be nearer than one and one-third Diameters, on centers, instead of one Diameter, on account of the projection of their bases, and in the Ionic, Corinthian, and Composite Orders, not nearer than one and one-half Diameters, on account of the projection of their Capitals. The Intercolumniation of Coupled Columns is accordingly one-third or one-half of a Diameter, or even a little more, to prevent the Bases or Caps from actually touching. As this brings them eight-sixths Diameters, or nine-sixths Diameters, on centers, the Ionic and Corinthian dentils, which are one-sixth Diameter on centers, come exactly on the axis of the columns. This occurs also with the dentils of Vignola's Composite Order, which are one-fourth Diameter on centers, since nine-sixths Diameters equals six-fourths Diameters, and there is just room for five dentils over the Intercolumniation. But since the Corinthian Modillions are four-sixths of a Diameter on centers, and the shafts of Coupled Columns are nine-sixths Diameters on centers, it is necessary to widen each of the two caissons between the Modillions by one-twelfth Diameter, and increase the width of the Dentils and Interdentils by one-eighth, making the Dentils one-eighth of a Diameter in width instead of one-ninth, and the Interdentils one-sixteenth of a Diameter instead of one-eighteenth. $[\frac{1}{9} \times 1\frac{1}{8} = \frac{1}{8};\ \frac{1}{18} \times 1\frac{1}{8} = \frac{1}{16}.]$

So also the Pycnostyle Intercolumniation is made one and one-fourth Diameters instead of one Diameter (i. e., two and one-fourth Diameters on centers, instead of two) to avoid crowding. The ancients thought that even the Systyle columns, with an Intercolumniation of two Diameters, came too near together, and preferred what they called the *Eustyle Intercolumniation,* of two and one-half Diameters (or three and one-half Diameters on centers, in place of three Diameters). But the moderns prefer to make the Eustyle Intercolumniation two and one-third Diameters (setting the columns three and one-third Diameters, on centers), as this brings every Column in Ionic and Corinthian colonnades exactly under a Dentil, and every alternate one just under a Modillion, the Dentils being one-sixth of a Diameter on centers, and the Modillions two-thirds of a Diameter.

Fig. 153

The wider Intercolumniations are preferable, obviously, when the columns are small, since otherwise it might be difficult to get between them, and the Systyle, or even the Pycnostyle, when the columns are very large, since otherwise it might be difficult to find stone architraves long enough to span the interval. But the ancients used Tuscan Columns chiefly with wooden architraves, setting them as much as seven Diameters apart, which is called the *Tuscan Intercolumniation*, and which makes the space between the columns about square. In modern times, also, an arrangement of coupled columns has been employed, called *Areosystyle*, the columns being set half a Diameter apart, and the space between the pairs of columns made three and one-half Diameters. This is greater than the Diastyle Intercolumniation and less than the Areostyle by half a Diameter. From the axis of one pair of columns to that of the next pair the distance is six Diameters. If in a Systyle Colonnade, with the columns three Diameters on centers, the alternate columns are moved along until they nearly touch the intervening ones, the result is an Areostyle Colonnade. This was first used by Perrault in the Eastern Colonnade of the Louvre, Fig. 153.

In actual practice these rules for Intercolumniation are seldom exactly followed.

DORIC INTERCOLUMNIATIONS—PLATE XVIII

In the Doric Order, since the Columns come exactly under the Triglyphs and the Triglyphs are one and one-fourth Diameters on centers, as on edges (the width of the Triglyph being one-half of a Diameter and that of the Metopes three-fourths of a Diameter), the distance of the Columns on centers must needs be a multiple of one and one-fourth Diameters.

This makes the coupling of Doric Columns difficult, since, even if the Bases touch, the distance between axes is still one and one-third Diameters, which is more than that of the Triglyphs by one-twelfth of a Diameter. This slight discrepancy can, however, be got over by making each Base a trifle narrower, or the Triglyphs and Metopes a trifle wider, or by putting the Columns *not* exactly under the Triglyphs, or by employing all these devices at once.

If the Columns are set under alternate Triglyphs so that there is one Triglyph over the intervening space, their distance apart on centers is two and one-half Diameters. The Intercolumniation is then one and one-half Diameters, and is said to be *Monotriglyph*. This is the most common arrangement. But if the scale is small, it is usual, at least at the principal entrance of a building, to have two Triglyphs over the opening, the Columns being three and three-fourths Diameters on centers. The Intercolumniation is then two and three-fourths Diameters, and is called *Ditriglyph*. Still wider spacing is employed when the Architraves are of wood.

When two, four, six, eight, ten, or twelve Columns are used in a Colonnade or Portico, it is said to be *Distyle*, *Tetrastyle*, *Hexastyle*, *Octastyle*, *Decastyle*, or *Dodecastyle*, according to the Greek numerals. Examples are found at Argos, Assos, Thoricus, and Pæstum of façades with an odd number of columns, three, five, seven, and nine, a column instead of an intercolumniation coming on the axis, giving *tristyle*, *pentastyle*, *heptastyle*, and *enneastyle* porticos. But in all these cases the entrances were apparently on the sides of the buildings, where there was an even number of columns.

SUPERPOSITION—PLATE XVIII

SUPERPOSITION is the placing of one Order above another, as in the Roman Amphitheaters and in many modern buildings of several stories. The more solid forms of the Tuscan and Doric are naturally placed below, and the Ionic and Corinthian above. The Composite is sometimes placed below the Corinthian, as being more vigorous. But in high buildings it is generally placed on the top story, its large details being better seen at a distance than are those of the more delicate Order.

Even when the same Order is employed in the different stories it is advisable to have the upper Columns of smaller diameter than those below, and all the dimensions diminished accordingly, for the sake of lightness. But it is still more so when different Orders are superposed, for otherwise the Doric and Corinthian stories would overpower the Tuscan and Ionic ones beneath (Plate XVIII, A). It is usual, accordingly, to make the lower diameter of each Shaft equal to the upper diameter of the Shaft below it, as if they were all cut from a single piece of tapering stone (Plate XVIII, B). This makes the scale employed in the second story five-sixths of that used in the first; in the third, twenty-five thirty-sixths, or about two-thirds; in the fourth, about three-fifths, and in the fifth, about one-half, if the Five Orders are employed in regular sequence; this makes the relative height of the Orders in the successive stories to be as 7, $6\frac{2}{3}$, $6\frac{1}{4}$, $5\frac{5}{6}$, and 5, very nearly. The actual height of the stories themselves may be somewhat modified by the use of plinths and pedestals.

This system of Superposition makes the distance apart of the Columns in each story, when expressed in terms of their own Diameter, six-fifths of that in the story below. A Eustyle Intercolumniation in one story thus exactly produces a Diastyle Intercolumniation in the story above, and a Doric Monotriglyph Intercolumniation, a Systyle (Plate XVIII, F).

$$(\tfrac{6}{5} \times 3\tfrac{1}{3} = 4; \ \tfrac{6}{5} \times 2\tfrac{1}{2} = 3)$$

Coupled Columns set one and one-third Diameters apart, on centers, in one story, are, in the story above, one and three-fifths Diameters o. c., and in the third story nearly two Diameters o. c. This does very well for

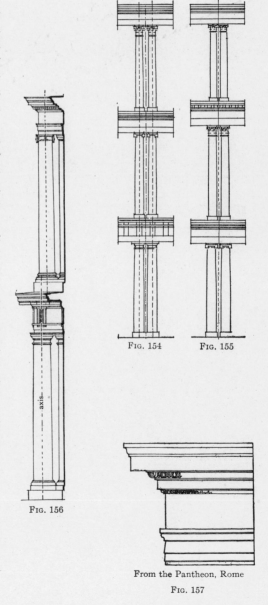

FIG. 154   FIG. 155

FIG. 156

From the Pantheon, Rome

FIG. 157

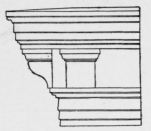

From the Fourth Order of the Collosseum

FIG. 158

From the Villa Caprarola. By Vignola

FIG. 159

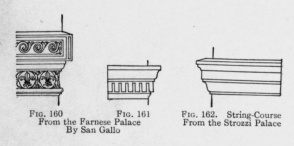

FIG. 160   FIG. 161   FIG. 162. String-Course
From the Farnese Palace   From the Strozzi Palace
By San Gallo

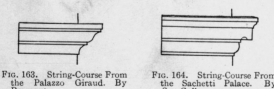

FIG. 163. String-Course From   FIG. 164. String-Course From
the Palazzo Giraud. By   the Sachetti Palace. By
Bramante   San Gallo

a sequence of Doric, Ionic, and Corinthian, Fig. 154. But if the lower Columns are Ionic or Corinthian those above had better be set nearer together, the axis of the Intercolumniation only being preserved, Fig. 155.

With this exception, Superposed Columns are set so that their axes are in the same vertical line, when seen in elevation. But in profile, as seen in section, the upper ones are set back, the wall against which they stand generally growing thinner as it goes up, Fig. 156. Since the Columns themselves also grow smaller, it would not do to leave too much space behind them. The slightly pyramidal effect that this gives to a building of several stories is of value, preventing it from looking top-heavy and high-shouldered (Plate XVIII, C).

OTHER CORNICES AND STRING-COURSES

The Five Orders worked out by Vignola are generally accepted as a standard, though they are seldom exactly followed in practice, modern as well as ancient examples exhibiting a great variety in the forms and proportions of the parts. But familiarity with them is of great service in designing, since they can safely be employed on all ordinary occasions, and in the earlier stages of architectural composition. Other types of nearly equal merit have been published by Alberti, Palladio, Serlio, Scamozzi, Sir William Chambers, and others, and a great variety of cornices, both with and without friezes and architraves, have been employed in ancient and modern times to crown and protect walls that were not decorated with columns or pilasters.

Many of these show Blocks or Modillions without any Dentil Course below, as on Palladio's Composite Cornice, and in many of them the Dentil Course is plain, forming what is called an *Uncut Dentil Course*, Fig. 157. In others, the brackets that support the Corona are brought down so as to occupy the Frieze, Fig. 158. The most important of these is Vignola's so-called *Cantilever Cornice* used by him at Caprarola, Fig. 159. It seems to have been suggested by the Mutules and Triglyphs of his Mutulary Doric.

Cornices, and indeed full Entablatures, are often used as String-Courses to separate stories, as in the Roman Amphitheaters. But it is customary to use, instead, a lighter form, of small projection, somewhat like the cap of a pedestal, in which the Cymatium and Bed Mold are often omitted, and the Corona itself sometimes diminished to a mere fillet, Figs. 160 to 164.

International Textbook Company,
Scranton, Pa.   1902

PRINTED IN U.S.A.

THE AMERICAN VIGNOLA

PLATE XI

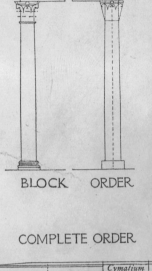

BLOCK   ORDER

COMPLETE ORDER

PLAN OF ENTABLATURE   LOOKING UP

Cymatium
Corona
Modillion Band

2 ½ D

Abacus.
Lip
Bell

7/6 D

Astragal

8 ⅓ DIAMETERS

SHAFT

ENTASIS

10 DIAMETERS

⅓

STRAIGHT

½ D

Plinth

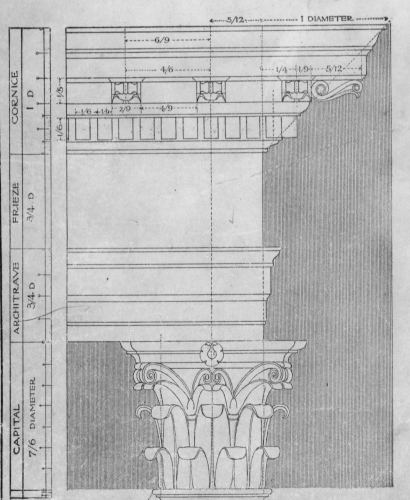

ELEVATION OF ENTABLATURE

CAPITAL	ARCHITRAVE	FRIEZE	CORNICE
7/6 DIAMETER	3/4 D	3/4 D	1 D

5/12   1 DIAMETER

6/9
4/6   1/4 1/9 5/12
1/6 1/9 2/9   4/9

CORINTHIAN ORDER

International Textbook Company
Scranton Pa.   19095

PRINTED IN U.S.A

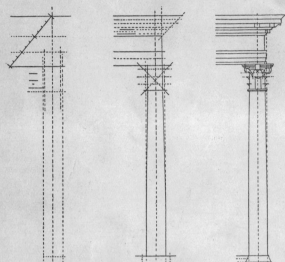

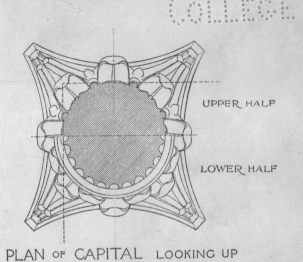

UPPER HALF

LOWER HALF

PLAN OF CAPITAL LOOKING UP

PERSPECTIVE VIEW

DRAWN TO THE SCALE
OF ORDER IN PLATE **XI**

THE AMERICAN VIGNOLA

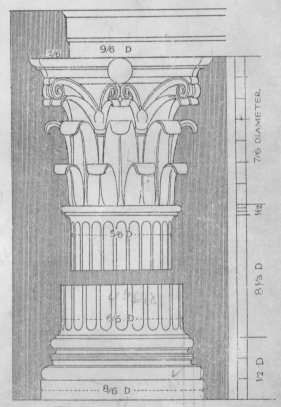

2/6   9/6 D

7/6 DIAMETER

1/2

5/6 D

8⅓ D

6/6 D

1/2 D

8/6 D

ELEVATION OF CAPITAL AND BASE

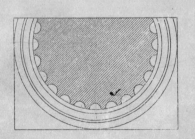

PLAN OF BASE

PLATE X

Copyright, 1902, by William R. Ware
Copyright, 1904, by International Textbook Company
8-311-I L T 153 §11

MOULDINGS

CYMA REVERSA

QUIRKED CYMA REVERSA

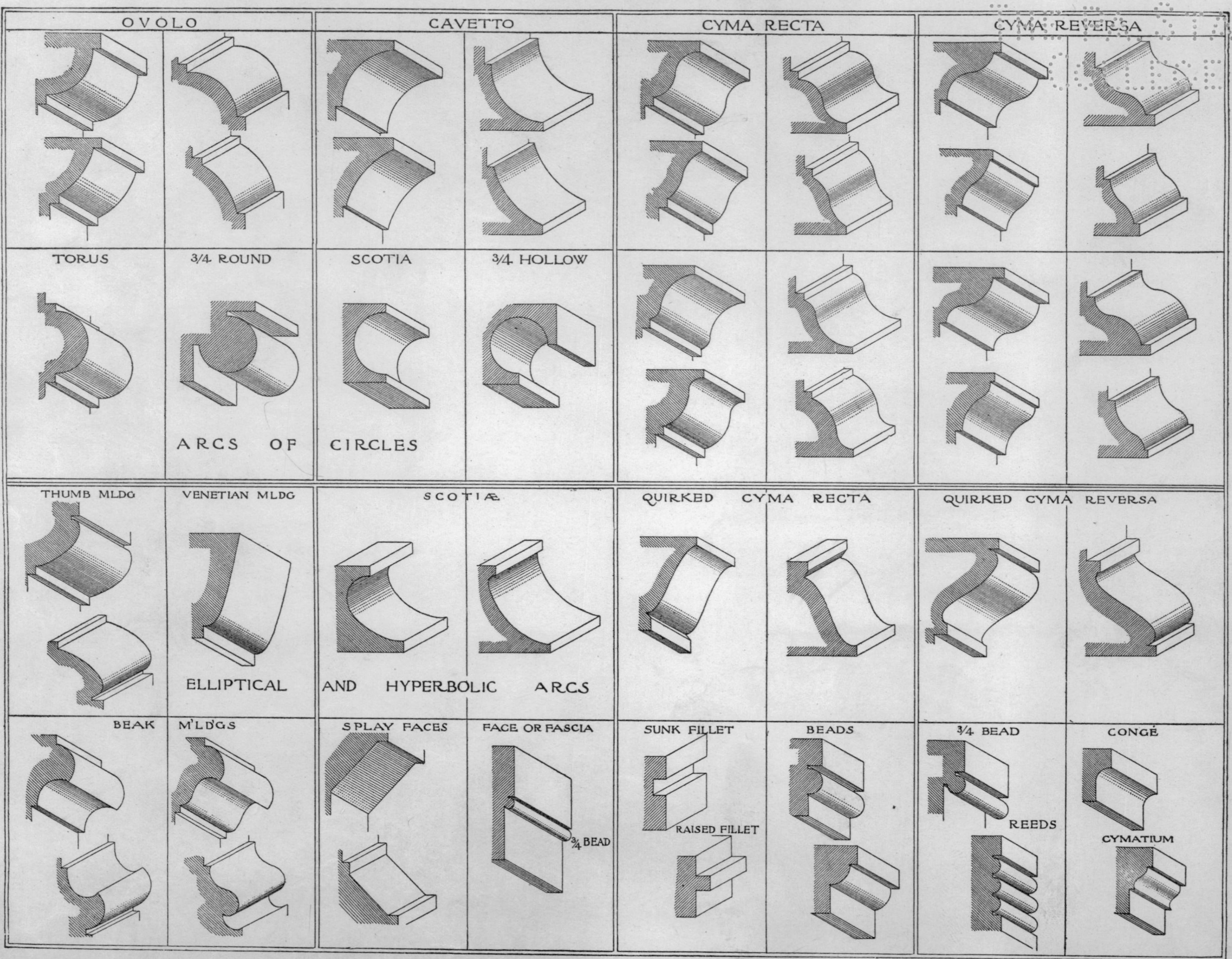

CONGÉ

CYMATIUM

¾ BEAD

REEDS

CYMA RECTA

CYMA RECTA

BEADS

QUIRKED CYMA

SUNK FILLET

RAISED FILLET

CAVETTO

¾ HOLLOW

SCOTIA

SCOTIA

ARCS OF CIRCLES

HYPERBOLIC ARCS

FACE OR FASCIA

¾ BEAD

SPLAY FACES

OVOLO

¾ ROUND

ARCS OF CIRCLES

VENETIAN MLDG.

ELLIPTICAL AND HYPERBOLIC

M'LDGS

TORUS

THUMB MLDG.

BEAK

PLATE 1

International Textbook Company,
Scranton, Pa.

THE AMERICAN VIGNOLA

right 1902, by William R. Ware
1904, by International Textbook Company

618H   8-311—I. L. T 153   § 11

19095

PRINTED IN U S A

THE AMERICAN VIGNOLA

COMPARISON OF THE ORDERS

TYPE OF ORDER	NAMES OF FEATURES		GREEK DORIC	TUSCAN	DORIC	IONIC	CORINTHIAN COMPOSITE	PERSPECTIVE VIEW
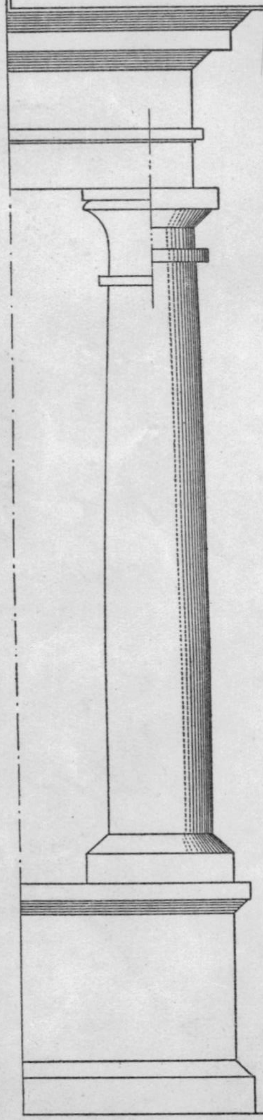 ENTABLATURE 1/4 to 1/5	CORNICE	CYMATIUM / CORONA / BED MOULD	1/2	3/4	3/4	7/8	1	FROM WITHOUT
	FRIEZE	TÆNIA	3/4	1/2	3/4	6/8	3/4	
	ARCHITRAVE		3/4	1/2	1/2	5/8	3/4	
		(total)	2	1¾	2	2¼	2½	
COLUMN 1	CAPITAL	ABACUS / ECHINUS / NECKING / ASTRAGAL	1/2	1/2	1/2	1/3 [1/2]	7/6	FROM WITHIN
	SHAFT		4·6	7 6	8 7	9 8	10 8⅓	
	BASE	CINCTURE / BASE MOULD / PLINTH	NONE	1/2	1/2	1/2	1/2	
PEDESTAL 1/3	CAP	CORONA / BED MOULDING	NO PEDESTAL BUT THREE STEPS THE STYLOBATE					
	DIE							
	BASE	BASE MOULD / PLINTH						

PEDESTAL [VIGNOLA] 1/3

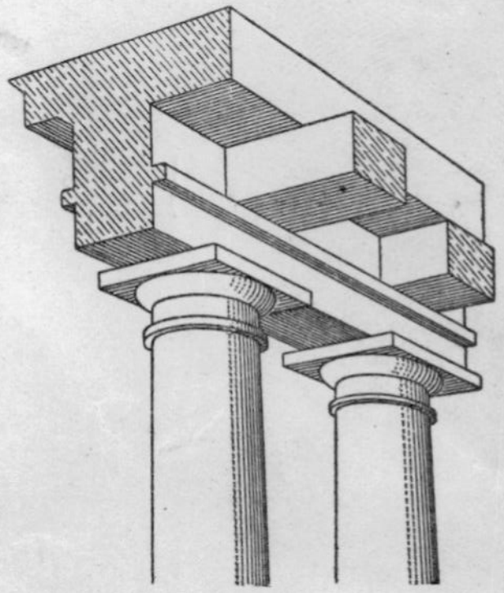

THE CAP IS ONE NINTH THE HEIGHT OF THE PEDESTAL

THE BASE IS TWO NINTHS THE HEIGHT OF THE PEDESTAL

PLATE II

International Textbook Company
Scranton, Pa. 19095
PRINTED IN U.S.A.

TUSCAN ORDER

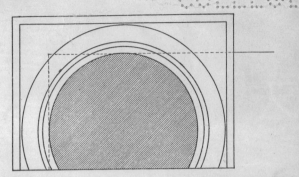

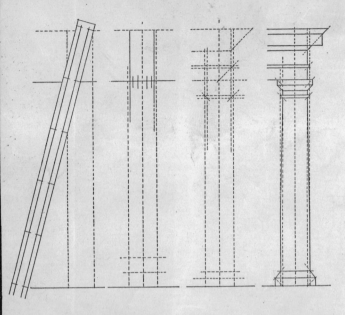

International Textbook Company.
Scranton, Pa.   1909

PLAN OF CAPITAL LOOKING UP

PERSPECTIVE VIEW

DRAWN TO THE SCALE
OF ORDER IN PLATE IV

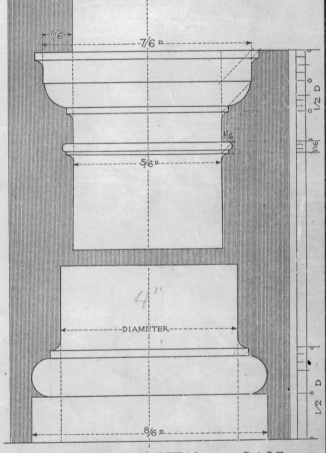

1/6

7/6 D

1/2 D

1/6

5/6 D

4"

DIAMETER

8/6 D

1/2 D

ELEVATION OF CAPITAL AND BASE

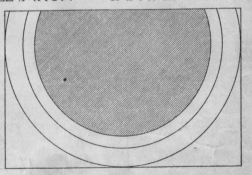

PLAN OF BASE

THE AMERICAN VIGNOLA

PLATE III

Copyright, 1902, by William R. Ware
Copyright, 1904, by International Textbook Company

DORIC ORDER

International Textbook Company
Scranton. Pa.   19095

PRINTED IN U.S.A.

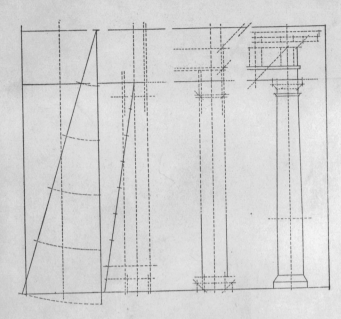

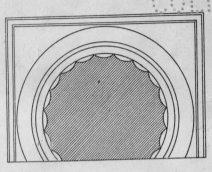

PLAN OF CAPITAL

PERSPECTIVE VIEW

DRAWN TO THE SCALE OF ORDER IN PLATE **VI**

THE AMERICAN VIGNOLA

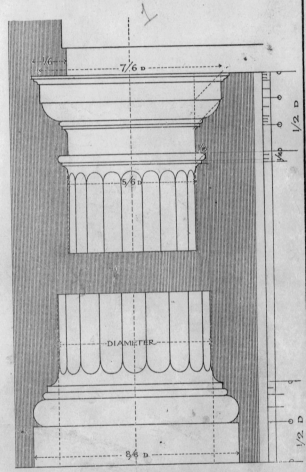

ELEVATION OF CAPITAL AND BASE

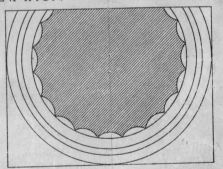

PLAN OF BASE

PLATE V

Copyright, 1902, by William R. Ware
Copyright, 1904, by International Textbook Company

DORIC ORDER

International Textbook Company, Scranton, Pa. 19095

PRINTED IN U.S.A.

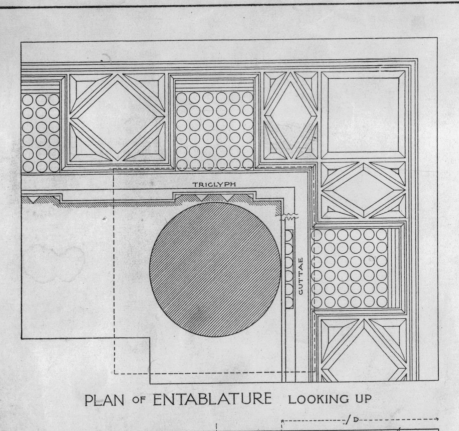

TRIGLYPH

CUTTAE

PLAN OF ENTABLATURE LOOKING UP

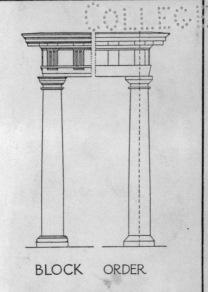

BLOCK ORDER

COMPLETE ORDER

Cymatium	
Corona	
Mutules	
Bed Mould	
Metope	
Triglyphs	2 D
Taenia	
Abacus	
Echinus	
Necking	
Astragal	

SHAFT — 7 DIAMETERS — ENTASIS

STRAIGHT ⅓

8 DIAMETERS

Torus
Plinth

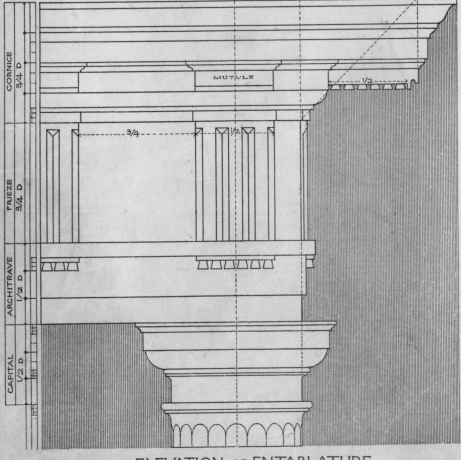

CORNICE 3/4 D

FRIEZE 3/4 D

ARCHITRAVE 1/2 D

CAPITAL 1/2 D

MUTULE

3/4   1/2

1/2

/ D

ELEVATION OF ENTABLATURE

THE AMERICAN VIGNOLA

PLATE VI

Copyright, 1902, by William R. Ware
Copyright, 1904, by International Textbook Company

DORIC ORDER [DENTICULATED]

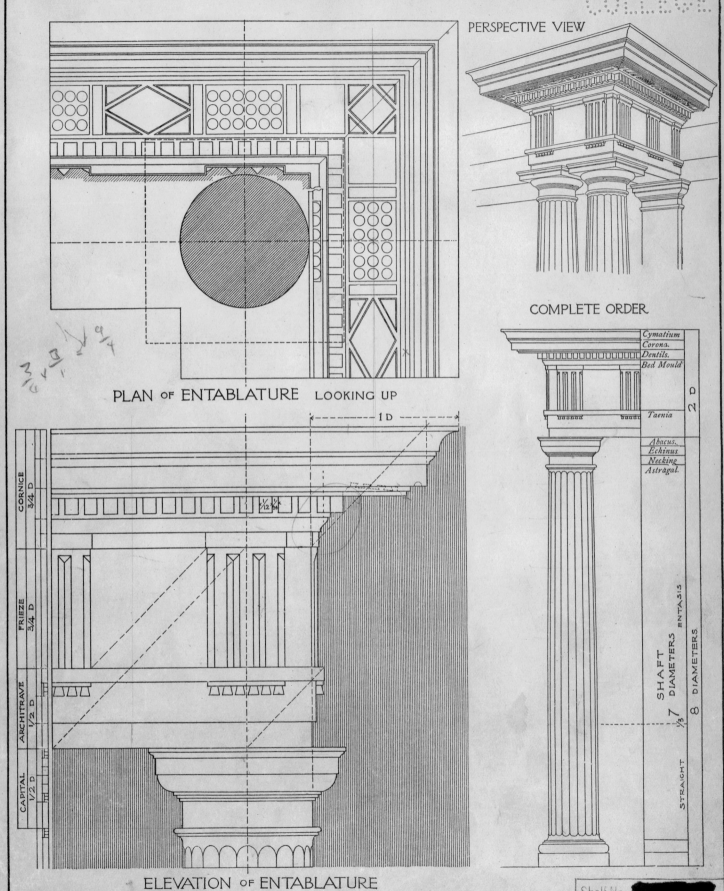

PERSPECTIVE VIEW

PLAN of ENTABLATURE LOOKING UP

COMPLETE ORDER

ELEVATION of ENTABLATURE

THE AMERICAN VIGNOLA

CORNICE 3/4 D

FRIEZE 3/4 D

ARCHITRAVE 1/2 D

CAPITAL 1/2 D

Cymatium
Corona.
Dentils.
Bed Mould
Taenia
Abacus.
Echinus.
Necking
Astragal.

SHAFT
7 DIAMETERS
ENTASIS
STRAIGHT
8 DIAMETERS.

1 D

2 D

International Textbook Company.
Scranton, Pa. 10095

PRINTED IN U.S.A.

Copyright, 1902, by William R. Ware

PLATE VII

IONIC ORDER

PLAN OF CAPITAL

THE AMERICAN VIGNOLA

8/6

1 DIAMETER

VIGNOLA'S BASE

1/3 D

1/2 D

4/6
5/6
6/6
9/6

1/2 D

8/6 D

ELEVATION OF CAPITAL BASE

PLAN OF BASE

PERSPECTIVE VIEW

DRAWN TO THE SCALE OF ORDER IN PLATE IX

International Textbook Company, Scranton Pa " 1905

PRINTED IN U.S.A.

PLATE VIII

Copyright, 1902, by William R. Ware
Copyright, 1904, by International Textbook Company
8.211-J L T 153 8 11

IONIC ORDER

PLAN of ENTABLATURE LOOKING UP

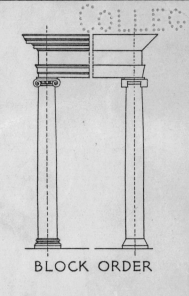

BLOCK ORDER

COMPLETE ORDER

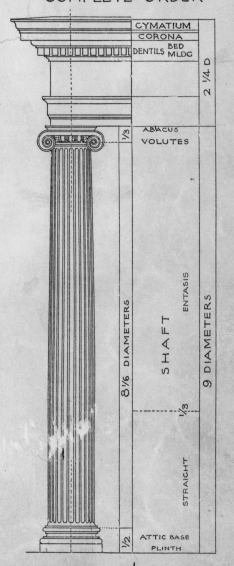

CYMATIUM
CORONA
DENTILS BED MLDG
2 1/4 D

ABACUS
VOLUTES

8 1/2 DIAMETERS

SHAFT
ENTASIS

9 DIAMETERS

STRAIGHT

ATTIC BASE
PLINTH

THE AMERICAN VIGNOLA

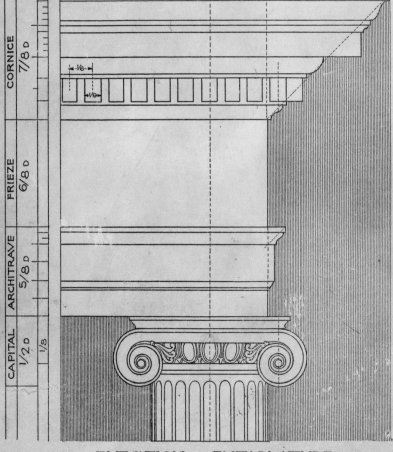

CAPITAL	ARCHITRAVE	FRIEZE	CORNICE
1/2 D	5/8 D	6/8 D	7/8 D
1/3			

5/12   7/8

1/6

1/9

ELEVATION of ENTABLATURE

International Textbook Company
Scranton. Pa.   1905

PRINTED IN U.S.A.

PLATE IX

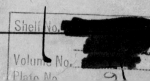

COMPOSITE ORDER

AFTER VIGNOLA

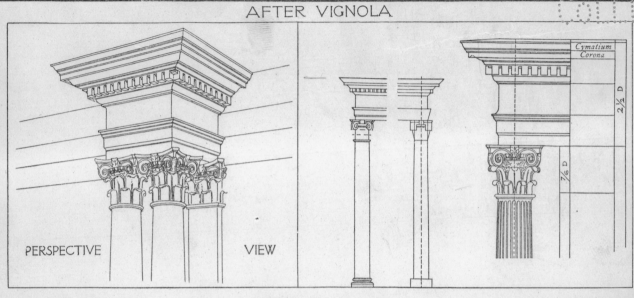

PERSPECTIVE   VIEW

Cymatium
Corona

2½ D

⅞ D

AFTER PALLADIO

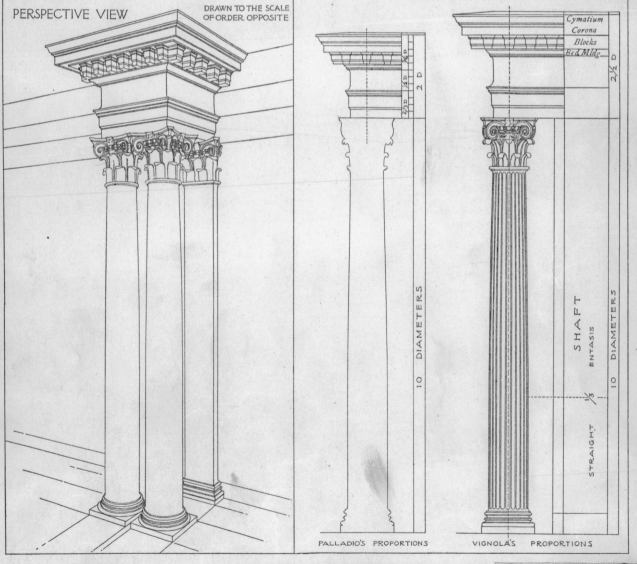

PERSPECTIVE VIEW   DRAWN TO THE SCALE OF ORDER OPPOSITE

Cymatium
Corona
Blocks
Bed Mldg.

2½ D

2½ D · ¼ D · ⅞ D

2 D

10 DIAMETERS

SHAFT

ENTASIS ⅓

STRAIGHT

10 DIAMETERS

PALLADIO'S PROPORTIONS   VIGNOLA'S PROPORTIONS

International Textbook Company
Scranton, Pa.
1905

PRINTED IN U.S.A.

THE AMERICAN VIGNOLA

PLATE XII

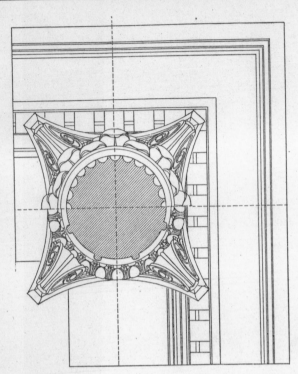

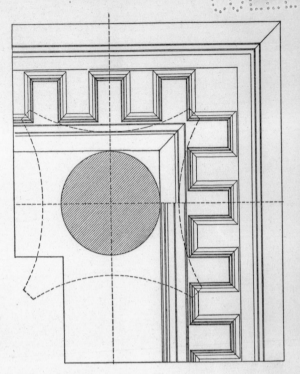

PLAN of ENTABLATURES LOOKING UP

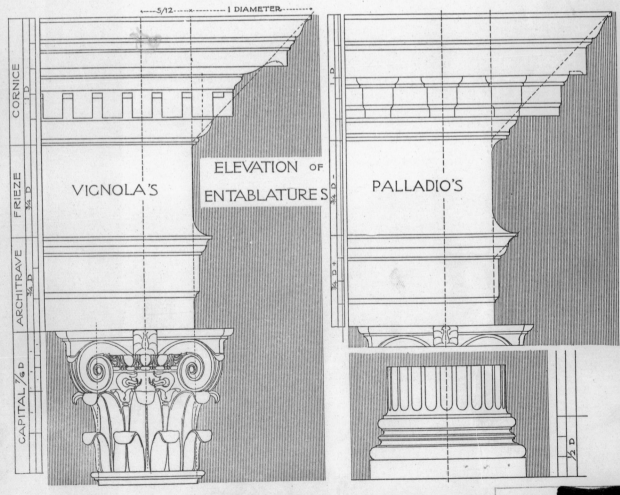

ELEVATION of ENTABLATURES

VIGNOLA'S

PALLADIO'S

5/12 — 1 DIAMETER

CORNICE 1 D

FRIEZE ¾ D

ARCHITRAVE ¾ D

CAPITAL ⅞ D

PLATE XIII

International Textbook Company
Scranton, Pa. 19095

PRINTED IN U.S.A.

Copyright, 1902, by William R. Ware
Copyright, 1904, by International Textbook Company

8-311-1 L T 153 § 11

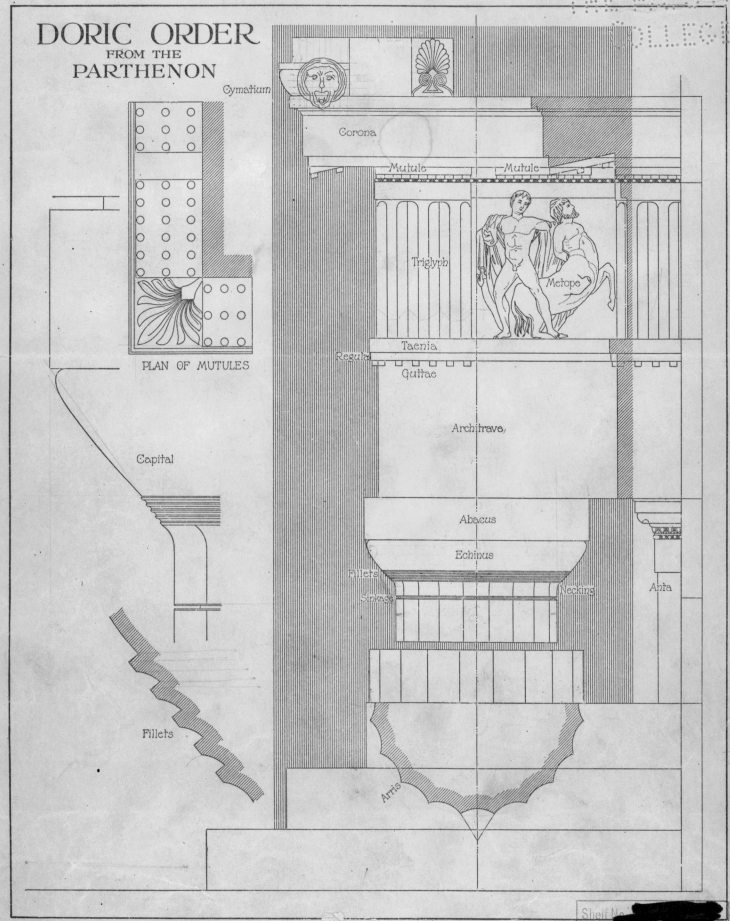

DORIC ORDER
FROM THE
PARTHENON

PLAN OF MUTULES

Cymatium

Capital

Fillets

Corona

Mutule — Mutule

Triglyph

Metope

Taenia

Regula

Guttae

Architrave

Abacus

Echinus

Fillets

Necking

Sinkage

Anta

Arris

International Textbook Company
Scranton, Pa. 1905

PRINTED IN U.S.A.

PLATE XIV

Copyright, 1902, by William R. Ware
Copyright, 1904, by International Textbook Company

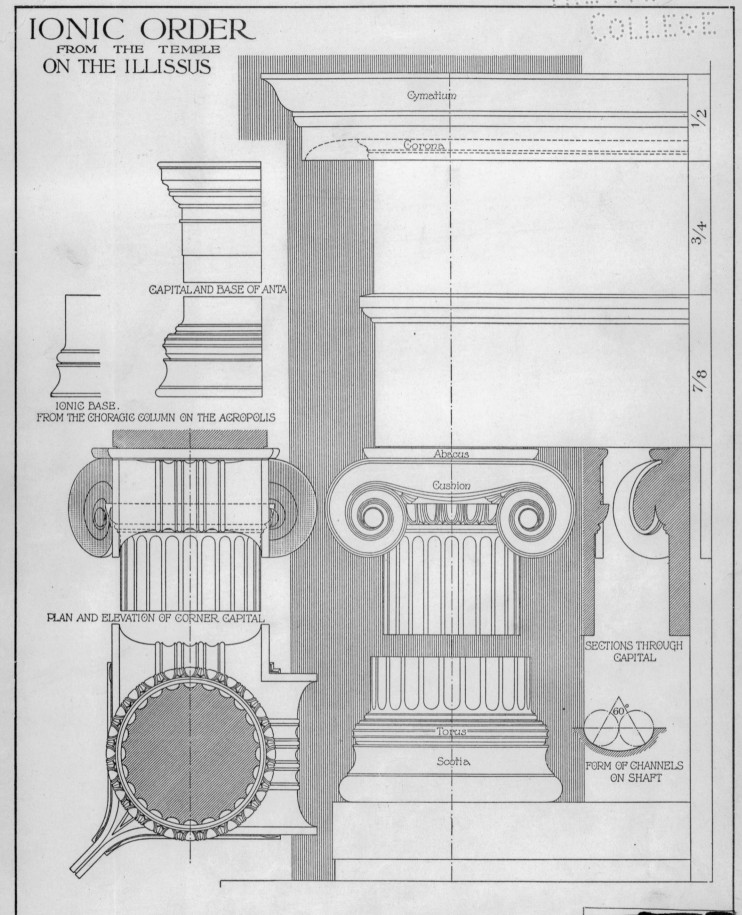

IONIC ORDER
FROM THE TEMPLE
ON THE ILLISSUS

CAPITAL AND BASE OF ANTA

IONIC BASE.
FROM THE CHORAGIC COLUMN ON THE ACROPOLIS

PLAN AND ELEVATION OF CORNER CAPITAL

Cymatium

Corona

1/2

3/4

7/8

Abacus

Cushion

Torus

Scotia

SECTIONS THROUGH CAPITAL

60°

FORM OF CHANNELS ON SHAFT

PLATE XV

International Textbook Company.
Scranton, Pa.   19005

PRINTED IN U.S.A.

Copyright, 1902, by William R. Ware
Copyright, 1904, by International Textbook Company

8-311-II. T 153 § 11

PEDESTALS AND PILASTERS

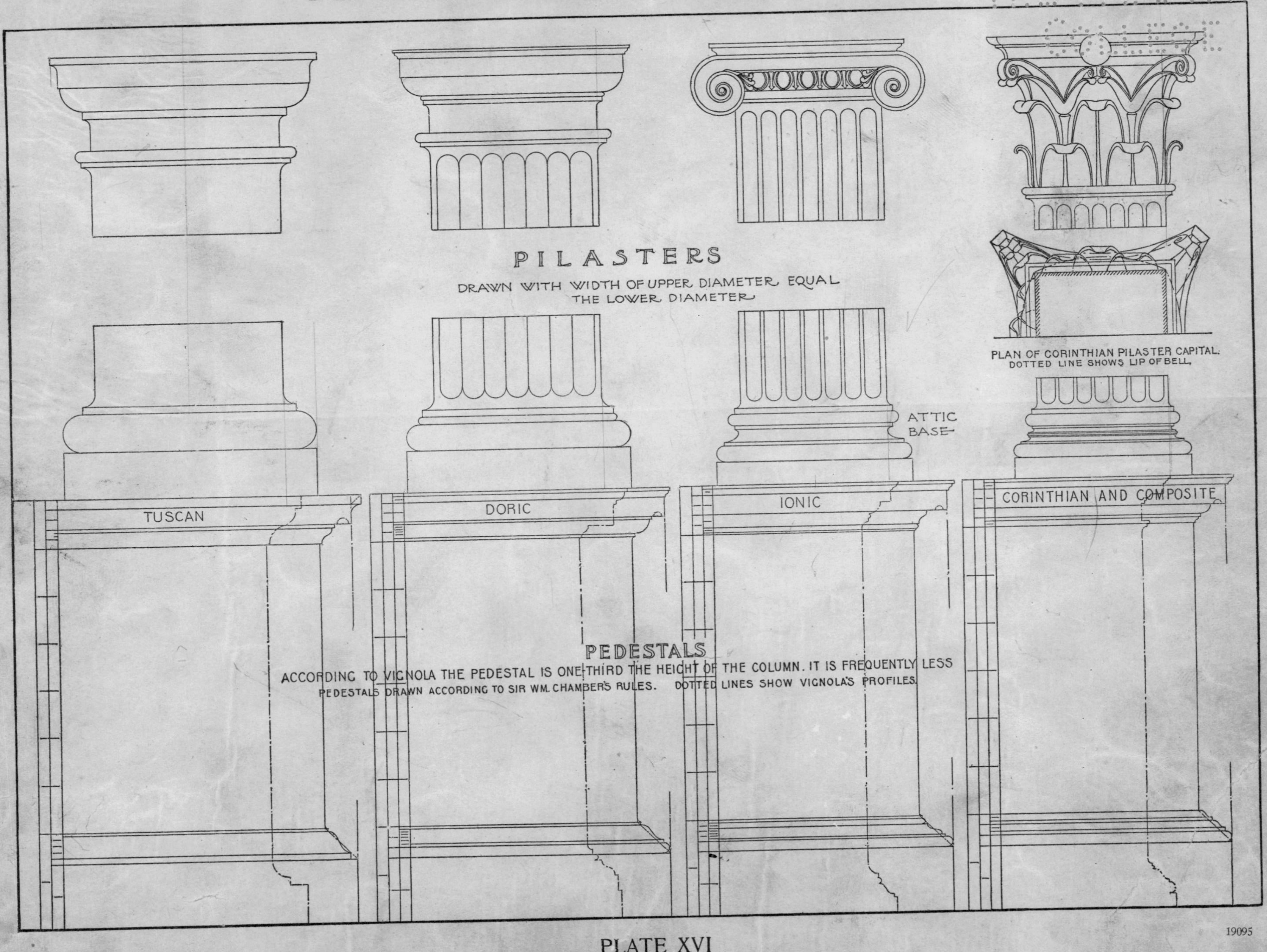

PLAN OF CORINTHIAN PILASTER CAPITAL.
DOTTED LINE SHOWS LIP OF BELL.

ATTIC
BASE

PILASTERS

DRAWN WITH WIDTH OF UPPER DIAMETER EQUAL
THE LOWER DIAMETER

CORINTHIAN AND COMPOSITE

IONIC

DORIC

TUSCAN

PEDESTALS

ACCORDING TO VIGNOLA THE PEDESTAL IS ONE-THIRD THE HEIGHT OF THE COLUMN. IT IS FREQUENTLY LESS.
DOTTED LINES SHOW VIGNOLA'S PROFILES.
PEDESTALS DRAWN ACCORDING TO SIR WM. CHAMBERS RULES.

PLATE XVI

THE AMERICAN VIGNOLA

International Textbook Company
Scranton, Pa.

Copyright, 1905, by William R. Ware
Copyright, 1904, by International Textbook Company

S-311-I-L T 153   § 11

19095

PEDIMENTS

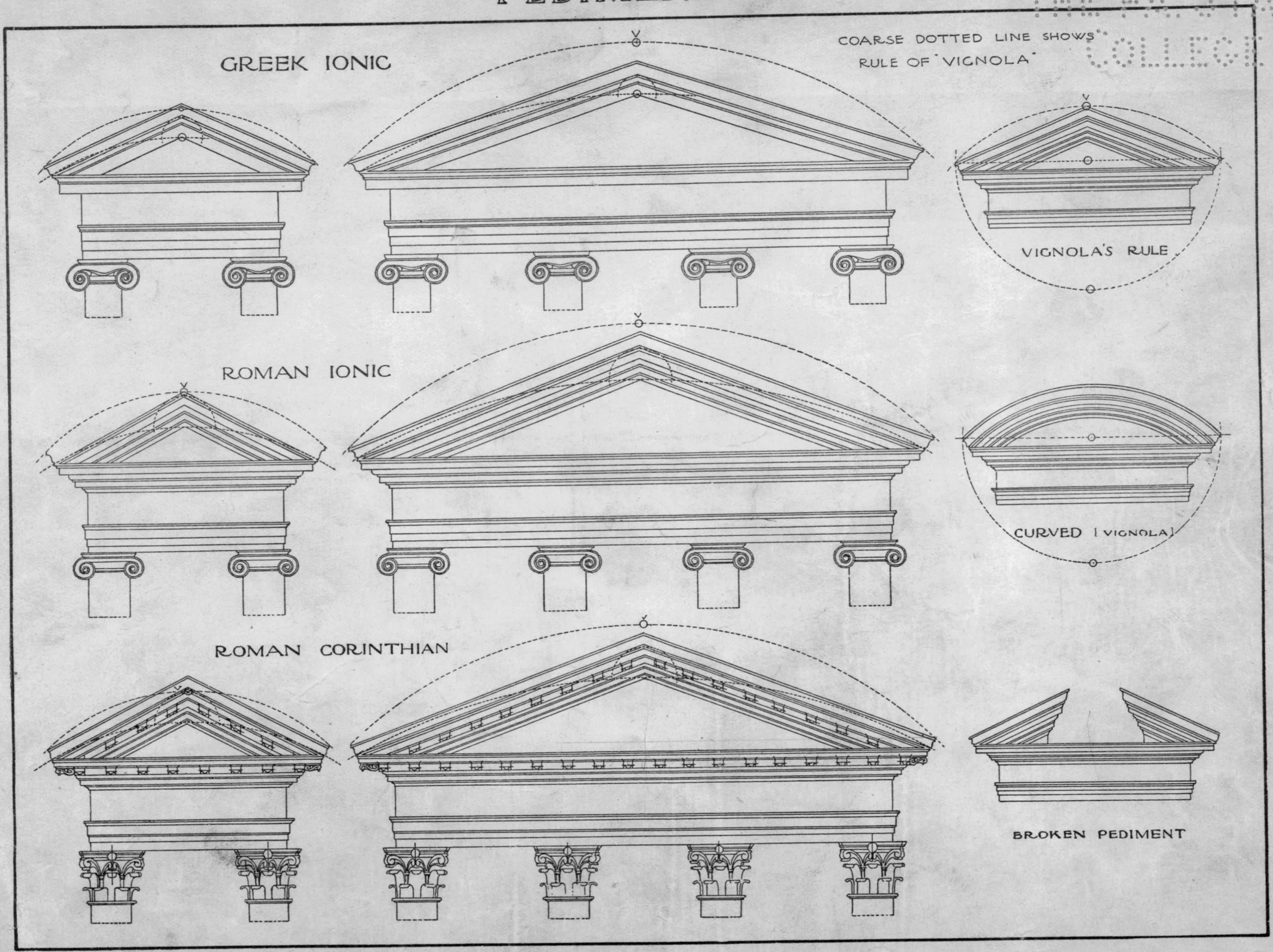

COARSE DOTTED LINE SHOWS "RULE OF VIGNOLA"

VIGNOLA'S RULE

CURVED (VIGNOLA)

BROKEN PEDIMENT

GREEK IONIC

ROMAN IONIC

ROMAN CORINTHIAN

PLATE XVII

8-311-ILT 153 § 11   PRINTED IN U.S.A   19095

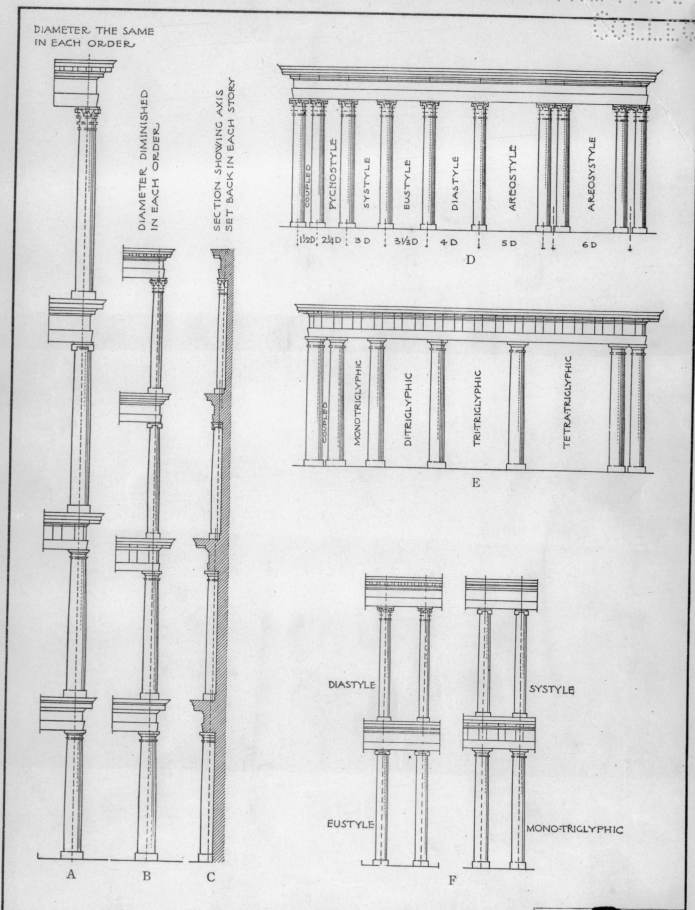

THE AMERICAN VIGNOLA.

DIAMETER THE SAME IN EACH ORDER

DIAMETER DIMINISHED IN EACH ORDER

SECTION SHOWING AXIS SET BACK IN EACH STORY

A   B   C

COUPLED   PYCNOSTYLE   SYSTYLE   EUSTYLE   DIASTYLE   AREOSTYLE   AREOSYSTYLE

1½ D   2¼ D   3 D   3⅓ D   4 D   5 D   6 D

D

COUPLED   MONOTRIGLYPHIC   DI·TRIGLYPHIC   TRI·TRIGLYPHIC   TETRA·TRIGLYPHIC

E

DIASTYLE   SYSTYLE

EUSTYLE   MONO·TRIGLYPHIC

F

PLATE XVIII

International Textbook Company
Scranton, Pa.   1905

PRINTED IN U.S.A.